WHAT IS DEEP PHILOSOPHY?

Philosophy from our inner depth

Loyev Books

WHAT IS DEEP PHILOSOPHY?

Philosophy from our inner depth

by
Ran Lahav

Loyev Books

Hardwick, Vermont, USA

https://dphilo.org/loyev-books

Text copyright @ 2021 by Ran Lahav

All Rights Reserved

Cover photograph © 2021 Ran Lahav

ISBN-13: 978-1-947515-10-9

Loyev Books

1165 Hopkins Hill Rd., Hardwick, Vermont 05843, USA

https://dphilo.org/loyev-books

Table of Contents

Foreword	vii
Part A: FIRST ENCOUNTER WITH DEEP PHILOSOPHY	1
Chapter 1: Glimpses of deep philosophy	3
Chapter 2: Moments of contemplation	16
Chapter 3: Reflections on the meaning of deep philosophy	24
Chapter 4: Experiential understanding	35
Chapter 5: Reveries on the broader horizons	44
Part B: ROOTS OF DEEP PHILOSOPHY	52
Chapter 6: The Deep Philosophy Group	54
Chapter 7: Historical roots	66
Part C: PILLARS OF DEEP PHILOSOPHY	77
Chapter 8: Summary of the seven pillars of deep philosophy	78
Chapter 9: Reflections on the pillars of deep philosophy	85
Part D: THE PRACTICE OF DEEP PHILOSOPHY	111
Chapter 10: The general setting	112
Chapter 11: Methods	119
Chapter 12: After the session	137

PREFACE

Deep Philosophy means doing philosophy from our inner depth. This is a philosophical-contemplative quest, and the Deep Philosophy Group is an international group of people devoted to this quest. By contemplating on fundamental aspects of life, we seek to relate to the foundation of human reality. By doing so from our inner depth, we seek to give voice to our deepest personal sensitivities and yearnings. By contemplating on texts from the history of philosophy, we seek to take part in the rich symphony of human voices throughout the ages. And by contemplating in togetherness with our companions, we seek to transcend the boundaries of our individual viewpoint and take part in a broader scope of humanity.

Deep Philosophy is the product of my personal search of four decades in search of a philosophy that would be intellectually responsible, yet personally deep and meaningful. I started this quest as a university student of philosophy, and later a university professor, yearning to explore the foundation of human reality, but unsatisfied with the remote abstractions of academic discourse. During those early years I was in a state of unrequited love – in love with the philosophical quest, but suffering from the coldness and intellectualism of the philosophy I knew. Yet, looking back now, I have to admit that I owe much to my academic studies and work, because they have given me crucial skills and knowledge which served as the intellectual foundation of future developments.

My exodus out of the academic world started when, as a young university professor, I encountered the field of so-called philosophical counseling, or more broadly philosophical practice. This small international movement at first excited me as a potential way of bringing philosophy and life together. I became internationally active in this movement, but after several years I realized that it was not what I was searching for. I wanted a philosophy that would deepen life, not tame it and satisfy it; a philosophy that would create inner transformation, not merely solve personal problems; one that would be true to the original philosophical mission to connect to the foundation of reality as far as humanly possible.

It took me a few more years to find my way. It started on a very small scale: At first, self-reflection workshops which I gave here and there; then a series online sessions that I organized with friends and colleagues; then experimental workshops, retreats, and online groups. Eventually a new framework of contemplative philosophy emerged, at first under the name "Philosophical Companionships" and later as "Deep Philosophy."

Only now did I feel that I finally reached what I had been seeking during decades of philosophical activity: A truly philosophical search for the foundation, personal, deep, contemplative, and in togetherness with my companions and with past thinkers. I was now ready to create, with the help of like-minded companions, the Deep Philosophy Group. In this international group we contemplate, explore new paths, and offer philosophical-contemplative sessions to others who seek too.

Importantly, Deep Philosophy is not a new invention. Nothing is completely new in the history of thought. The roots of Deep Philosophy can be found throughout the history of philosophy, from the practices of ancient Greek and Hellenistic thinkers, through the philosophical-poetic writings of German Romanticists and American Transcendentalists, to existentialist thinkers and beyond.

These historical roots testify that Deep Philosophy is a new branch of the age-old human tree of philosophical wisdom. It is certainly not an ultimate answer, either personally for me or for anybody else. As history shows us, philosophy is a historical polyphony of voices that keeps developing and acquiring new forms. It is my hope that Deep Philosophy will not petrify into a fixed doctrine, but will inspire other seekers to keep renewing the never-ending historical quest for wisdom and depth.

Ran Lahav
Vermont, USA, 2021

Part A

FIRST ENCOUNTER WITH DEEP PHILOSOPHY

It is not easy to give a systematic account of Deep Philosophy. Like many other human activities, Deep Philosophy is not one unitary thing. It grew out of a variety of personal experiences and yearnings, was guided by diverse insights and intuitions that gained prominence at different times, and was shaped by a network of considerations that arose in response to specific challenges.

Therefore, a systematic account of Deep Philosophy would necessarily be a retroactive interpretation, more like a simplified brochure for tourists than a faithful description of the actual lay of the land. Nevertheless, such an account, even if somewhat forced, could help shed light on the nature of Deep Philosophy, as long as it is understood to be an approximate sketch.

In this book I wish to present the main themes found in the evolving realm of Deep Philosophy, including its rich – and perhaps confusing – texture of experiences, ideas, and practices. My presentation will necessarily be somewhat fragmentary, although I believe that the fragments will add up to a more or less coherent whole.

The general landscape of Deep Philosophy can be divided into three main dimensions: First, the theoretical dimension which includes the basic concepts and principles on which the practice of Deep Philosophy is based. Second, the historical dimension, specifically its historical roots and sources of inspiration. And third, the dimension of practice, including its general methodological principles and repertoire of exercises and procedures.

Before delving in depth into each of these dimensions, a good starting point would be some preliminary glimpses of Deep Philosophy – experiences, observations, fragmentary ideas, metaphysical speculations – lightly organized according to content, but not forced into an artificial structure.

Chapter 1

GLIMPSES OF DEEP PHILOSOPHY

We can start appreciating the spirit of Deep Philosophy when we notice that it is intimately connected to certain precious experiences which many of us sometimes have in everyday moments. These experiences typically occur spontaneously. We may simply go about our ordinary life when suddenly they flutter in our awareness – in the form of a precious insight, or an understanding that seems to come to us from nowhere, or one that is accompanied by a sense of presence and realness. Often these experiences are too fleeting to attract our attention, but if we notice them, if we pay attention to their special qualities, then we are taking a first step towards Deep Philosophy. Because Deep Philosophy revolves around these special moments.

Bubbles of understanding

It happens sometimes in a small unexpected moment – in the midst of a conversation, at work, while taking a walk – that a "bubble" of insight rises into my awareness, like a bubble of air rising from the depth of a lake to the face of the water. It comes into my mind as if from elsewhere, like a silent whisper from an unknown depth of my being. I savor this new understanding and sense its preciousness. The bubble may be hardly noticeable, and the insight it brings me may be minor, yet it has a peculiar quality of special realness and significance.

And then I realize: Not everything that happens to me originates from the same place in my mind; not everything comes from my familiar self. There are hidden dimensions of my being, beyond the psychological structure which I call "I," that are sources of precious inspiration.

When thought is suspended

I sit down to read, and my mind, normally talkative, finds itself following the printed lines calmly and gently. The words of the text start floating within me with a special significance, and I listen to them quietly and notice their presence. My thoughts slow down, and a peculiar stillness descends over me, clear and tender. I now realize how noisy my mind had been. A new insight may appear in this marvelous stillness, barely describable in words but intensely present. It reveals new unnamable meanings, and I savor them.

It is as if a different source of understanding is thinking within me, deeper than my familiar thinking self. It is, perhaps, a hidden dimension of my being that gives birth to those new understandings, a hidden fountain beyond the usual confines of my mind, or a vast ocean of meanings that pours its precious waters into me.

Contemplation

My precious bubbles of understanding are often spontaneous: All of a sudden they rise into my awareness as if by themselves, like gifts from elsewhere, gently floating within me for a while and then vanishing. I cannot produce them at will, I can only prepare an inner space for them, a clearing in the forest of my mind, to receive them if they come.

I silence my inner commotion and quietly listen inside. I wait. I know I must be patient, but not completely passive. I have discovered that if I place a thought in this inner stillness and gently reflect on it, then sometimes a bubble of precious understanding emerges. A thought, if handled carefully, can serve as a seed of insights.

And now I am no longer a surprised recipient of unexpected understandings. I am intentionally shaping my inner attitude. This is called contemplating – silencing my thinking, opening an inner space of listening, placing in it a seed of understanding – a sentence, an idea, a text – and listening for a response from elsewhere.

Philosophical contemplation

I want to read a text in contemplation, to listen to it from my inner silence. But what kind of text should it be?

I could contemplate on a popular song, or a newspaper column, or a scientific article. Somehow, however, these texts would not elicit the proper inspiration. They are too concrete and specific for giving birth to deep precious understandings.

For contemplation, the words must relate to primordial meanings. They must point beyond specific facts and objects, to a realm of greater dimensions.

Such are words of philosophy, at least a deep kind of philosophy. A deep philosophical text deals with fundamental meanings.

Contemplating on a philosophical text is called philosophical contemplation. It means listening to basic meanings of human reality. Such meanings do not appear "inside" my mind – they are too primordial to be "mine" or "inside" me. They are from the greater reality that envelops me.

In philosophical contemplation I listen "through" a philosophical text to fundamental meanings. I quietly read the philosophical ideas while letting them speak within me, without imposing my opinions on them, without analyzing or agreeing or disagreeing. And, then, through those ideas I receive precious understandings rising from my depth and filling me with a powerful presence.

Deep Philosophy

After I experience philosophical contemplation, after I witness the intense precious presence of deep understandings, I wish to turn this into a regular practice and devote to it some of my time.

I may do so quietly by myself in my room. But I may also find several companions who want to practice philosophical contemplation together, whether because they have experienced what I have experienced, or because they are curious to try.

And now we are a group of philosophical contemplators. We meet periodically and contemplate together. We decide on certain procedures to follow and on a list of philosophical texts. We are a group now, a group of Deep Philosophy.

Contemplative exercises

At first our group wanted to contemplate freely, to simply open the hearts and minds and listen silently through the text to deep, fundamental meanings. But the mind does not open itself on its own. It is governed by rigid psychological thinking patterns. It is not as free as it might seem to be, because it is controlled by an automatic pilot called psychology.

We must push aside our psychological patterns and orient the mind towards deep inner listening, but this is not easy to do without appropriate techniques. We must use special exercises such as reading the text very slowly, or speaking in unusual ways, or forcing ourselves to listen to the sounds of the words as they reverberate in the room, or chanting a sentence over and over again until its ordinary meaning disintegrates, or formulating ideas in precise, rhythmic, poetic fashion.

All this may feel artificial at first, and even annoying and boring. But there is no way around it: If we want to break away from our usual thinking patterns, we must impose on the mind artificial constraints.

The contemplative session

We might wish to make Deep Philosophy a way of life, not limited to specific sessions at specific times during the week. We might think that the connection to our deepest experiences ought to remain with us always, in everything we do, an uninterrupted inner silence and precious realness. This, however, is an unrealistic aspiration. We have a life to live, and we cannot sit and contemplate all day long. Deep Philosophy does not mean abandoning life, but enriching life with a deeper dimension.

That is why we practice Deep Philosophy in sessions of one to two hours which nourish us for the rest of the week. For a limited period of time we step out of our everyday activities and immerse ourselves in philosophical ideas and fundamental meanings. When the session is over, the intense experience dissipates, yet our general awareness of the depth remains.

Here Deep Philosophy is like love. Loving does not mean overflowing with emotion every moment of the day. It also includes conversations and planning, solving problems, cleaning the house or cooking, as well as struggling and suffering together. Deep Philosophy is a kind of love – a love for the depth of reality. And just as lovers must nurture their love with periods of "quality time" of intense togetherness, so it is with Deep Philosophy. Our "quality time" is our contemplative sessions.

But although Deep Philosophy is inspired by love, it is not just a spontaneous pouring of the heart. If we want our yearning to transcend the prison of our normal psychology, we need techniques to do so. A session, therefore, is a structured sequence of exercises or techniques.

Many of our contemplative sessions are online. Using the Zoom platform, we meet on the computer screen, five to twelve participants from all over the world, and contemplate in togetherness for one or two hours once a week. When possible, we organize a Deep Philosophy retreat in a convenient geographical location and spend a weekend together. But regardless of the setting, the center of each Deep Philosophy session is always the same: contemplating in togetherness from our inner depth.

Thus, a contemplative session is an interval separated from the rest of the day or the week. It is a "clearing" in the daily "forest" of our busy activity. It serves, like the lovers' quality time, or like the shaman's sacred time, to intensify our encounter with fundamental reality. It is also analogous to a religious prayer – a short interval of time in which practitioners reconnect with a higher dimension.

Texts for text-contemplation

Philosophers throughout the ages intended their philosophies to express truths about life and reality. Indeed, that is what we find in a typical philosophical text: A theory about freedom or about knowledge, arguments for the existence of God or arguments against it, statements about the nature of beauty or of justice. But for us, in Deep Philosophy, a philosophical text is more than an intellectual statement. When we read a philosophical text with quiet attentiveness, it sometimes touches us deeply, inspires us, and awakens within us something more profound than mere impersonal thoughts. It is as if a hidden dimension of our being is awakened for a few moments.

At such moments, our philosophical text is more than a theory. It gives us not just intellectual ideas to examine in the abstract, not just a theory to analyze, but a living presence within us. We sense the text giving voice to hidden meanings, and we feel their realness and their precious presence.

This is the heart of text-contemplation, which is the central activity of Deep Philosophy sessions. It is a structured form of reading, composed of procedures or exercises that help to overcome our normal thinking patterns and to assume a contemplative state of mind of listening inwardly. Unlike ordinary ways of reading, in which we impose on the reading our reasoning and opinions, in text-contemplation we let the text speak within us. And when we do so, deep meanings appear in our awareness as if by themselves.

The experience of philosophical contemplation

As contemplators, we often experience deep meanings coming from the text with a special sense of intensity, realness, preciousness, and silent presence. We may sense that "something bigger than me" is thinking within, or that we are open to a broader reality.

These experiences indicate that what is happening within us at those moments is not ordinary. Our usual ways of thinking no longer dominate, and a dormant dimension of our being is awakened.

This additional dimension is what we call "inner depth." We experience our inner depth as a source of a special kind of understanding. In contemplation we do not think from our ordinary psychological mechanisms as we normally do, but from our inner depth. Hence the name "Deep Philosophy."

Inner depth

Inner depth is the "place" within me where the drama of contemplation takes place. When I contemplate, I think from my inner depth, I listen from it, I speak and communicate from it. Through the practice of contemplation I hope to awaken and cultivate my inner depth.

"Depth" is a metaphor, and quite a common one. In everyday language we may say "This is a deep book," or "She is a deep thinker," and likewise we can talk of a "deep emotion" or "deep relationship." It is not clear whether all these expressions have the same meaning, since everyday language is often lax and inconsistent. But in Deep Philosophy we use the notion of "depth" more specifically to refer to a dimension of our being where we experience primordial thinking and understanding.

As contemplators know, it is virtually impossible to describe our inner depth. It seems to be a dimension of myself that is not accessible to language, and therefore that is more primordial than our linguistic abilities. It is usually dormant and hidden, but when it awakens in contemplation, my thoughts are clear and tranquil and fully present, exuding a sense of precious realness. I "listen" inwardly and witness new surprising understandings rising in my depth. It is as if something greater than my usual self is thinking through me. In comparison to this marvel, my ordinary thinking feels dull and lifeless.

Inner depth, then, like a spring that pours out its water from the depth of the earth, is a fountain of primordial meanings that brings them to the visible surface of our awareness.

Philosophical abstaining

When we contemplate on a deep philosophical text and savor its ideas, we find ourselves in a peculiar situation: On the one hand, the text may touch us with a powerful sense of precious realness. On the other hand, we do not necessarily agree with the text or accept it as true. Indeed, the text may contradict another text that we find equally inspiring. How can we be equally touched by two contradictory ideas?

This seems perplexing as long as we treat the text's ideas as a theory, in other words as a statement about the way things are, and thus as being either true or false. Two different theories that portray the same object differently cannot both be correct.

This puzzlement is resolved when we realize that, during contemplation, a philosophical text moves us not because of its truth but because of its depth, not because of what it tells us about reality but because of the meanings that it reveals. We receive from the text not fundamental truths but fundamental meanings.

These fundamental meanings are elicited in our inner depth when we listen inwardly to the text. And when this happens, our powerful experience of realness tells us that we are relating intimately to something very real, even though we cannot pretend to know what exactly it is. It is as if these meanings were "sounds" or "voices" that somehow reach our "ears" without revealing to us where they came from, and whose voice they are.

But in order to "hear" these fundamental meanings, we must treat the text as a carrier of meanings, in other words, abstain from judgement about its truth as a theory. We must not agree or disagree with it, but treat it as expressing a certain human encounter with reality. Because the original writer of the text, just like we the contemplators, could not capture fundamental reality with his theories, but only "hear" the meanings that it elicited in his encounter with it.

History of text-contemplation

Text-contemplation has historical roots in various spiritual and wisdom traditions. One example is the practices of Stoic philosophers, in the ancient Hellenistic and Roman world, who contemplated on Stoic principles using exercises of writing, reading, imagining, and thinking. Another example is the ancient Christian practice of *Lectio Divina*, which was standardized in the 12th century by the Carthusian monk Guigo II. It consists of reading from the Holy Scriptures in a meditative way, while listening internally to divine meanings as they appear in the practitioner's mind.

Unlike those spiritual traditions, however, in Deep Philosophy we do not adhere to any doctrine, whether philosophical, religious, or other. Our texts are taken from all historical periods and approaches, since we seek the rich polyphony of human voices, not a single authoritarian teaching. We typically use in each session an excerpt of 1-2 pages taken from a larger philosophical work. Especially effective are those excerpts that are concise and even poetic, and that deal with human situations such as love, authenticity, or longing. For a series of sessions we might select a series of historical texts that express a variety of viewpoints on the same topic. For us, those different viewpoints complement each other like different musical instruments in a concert.

Voices of human reality

In Deep Philosophy we strive to connect to the depth of human reality as intimately as humanly possible. We do not seek to theorize about the depth – that would mean looking at it from the perspective of an external observer, and thus objectifying it and turning it into a thing to be observed, independent from the thinking philosopher. It would also mean objectifying ourselves as subjects, pretending that we are a "thing" that thinks (to use Descartes' words).

We want to get in touch with reality before it is objectified through thought and language, before the subject-object distinction appears, before our psychological thinking mechanisms impose their patterns. For this purpose, no description that is "about" reality would work, no theory that tries to represent reality or capture it with its statements.

We call this primordial dimension "voices of human reality." This expression indicates several things:

First, it indicates that we are not referring here to subjective experiences in our minds, but to the reality of which we are a part, the ocean in which we are a wave.

Second, the expression indicates that this primordial realm consists not of objects and facts, not even of words and concepts, but of the meanings that lie behind them. This is implied by the metaphor of "voices": A speaker's voice is not just a physical sound, but also the meaning that it carries.

"Voices" is a metaphor that refers to the dimension of basic meanings.

But third, the notion of "voices" also indicates that those primordial meanings are fluid and changing. This is because they emerge from our encounter with reality, and those encounters change as human situations change, both culturally and individually.

Fourth, the expression reminds us that these basic meanings reach us not as objects of our thought or experience, not as a content to grasp, but through direct inspiration like a tremor resonating in the mind. They are incarnated within us, echoing throughout our being.

How fundamental are these voices? Are they ultimate reality, like God? Obviously we cannot make this claim. As human beings we are limited in ways we cannot comprehend. We cannot understand what lies beyond our horizon. These voices are primordial within our human horizons, within the realms that are in principle accessible to us. That is why we call them "voices of human reality."

So what is Deep Philosophy?

If I had to define Deep Philosophy in a single sentence, I would say: In Deep Philosophy we contemplate on basic life-issues from our inner depth, in togetherness with our companions and with historical philosophical texts.

This formulation tells us, first, that Deep Philosophy is a form of philosophy. Like numerous philosophers throughout history, it explores fundamental aspects of life and reality. But it also tells us that Deep Philosophy involves a special kind of philosophizing. Unlike typical academic thinking, in which we think from our intellect, in Deep Philosophy we think from our inner depth, in other words we contemplate.

Furthermore, this formulation also tells us that Deep Philosophy is primarily a group activity, practiced in small groups of people. Unlike ordinary discussion groups, participants do not argue, judge, or express their opinions. Rather, they reflect in togetherness, resonating with each other like musicians improvising together, creating together a philosophical polyphony.

Lastly, this formulation tells us that in Deep Philosophy we relate to previous historical thinkers. Philosophy, in the Western sense of the term, is a long tradition. It is a historical discourse in which every thinker emerges from the background of previous thinkers, whether explicitly or implicitly, and continues the discourse into the future. No philosophizing can start from zero, nor can it be separated from its history. That is why in our sessions we contemplate on a historical philosophical text – not as an authority to follow, but as material to work with and resonate with, and as a starting point for developing our personal understandings.

Chapter 2

MOMENTS OF CONTEMPLATION

Individual text-contemplation

Quietly I open my book and contemplate on my daily text, my eyes gliding gently over the lines. The words of the famous philosopher float softly through my mind: freedom, soul, nature – and I listen to the silence that encompasses them. All is present now and pregnant with deep meanings, and I receive them gratefully even though I cannot grasp them fully in my mind. I know I should not try to analyze them or impose on them my interpretations. I let them speak within me as they please and I listen to their voices.

Do I agree with the text, or do I disagree?

But in the stillness of the moment there is no right or wrong, no agreement or disagreement. There are meanings floating like music in the air, and they do not ask for my opinion. Opinions may be right or wrong, theories may be correct or mistaken, but what speaks in me through these pages is altogether different. It does not try to declare or convince or describe matters of fact. Like a melody, it just is.

I know, of course, that the ancient writer who had written this text intended to write a theory. He believed he was making a statement about life – about the nature of freedom and the structure of the soul or the spirit – and he declared it to be true. But what does it matter what the writer believed he was doing? He did not own these meanings, he only recorded them on paper when they spoke in his mind.

Group contemplation

When I sit alone in my room, my solitary contemplations bring me the purest silence and the most profound personal insights. Yet, I also seek the company of my companions. I cherish the gentle fullness of contemplation in togetherness. And if they are not available nearby, we meet through video-conferencing online, despite the computer-screen that stands between us and the electronic interruptions. Together we read a paragraph, or recite a selected sentence over and over again, or give voice to our inner depth and resonate with each other.

Group contemplation is not as silent as solitary contemplation, and not as inward-looking. My companions' faces and words do not let me delve as fully in my inner depth. Yet, precisely because I am open to the voices of my companions and let them enrich my own voice, I am more than myself. I am now a voice in a chorus. I may not reach as deeply inside me, but I reach out beyond my boundaries, towards the broader realms of human reality.

The Centering Exercise

We assemble, nine participants, for a session of Deep Philosophy. Our facilitator greets the group and directly starts the session with a "centering exercise."

A centering exercise is a quick meditation to silence the mind and prepare it for the session. Here we will make the first step into the realm of contemplation, where our mind will gain some freedom from our usual thinking patterns and the psychological structures that try to govern it.

For this particular session our facilitator chose a centering exercise that uses the column of air as a metaphorical ladder that descends into our inner depth. She asks us to close our eyes, gently turn our attention inwards, and concentrate on our nose.

"We are now resting inside our nostrils," she says calmly, "and sensing the air as it flows inside and outside."

After three or four breaths, the facilitator instructs us to mentally go down to our mouth, stay there for a while, and sense the air flowing over the tongue. After three more breaths, we go further down to our throat, then along the column of air to the chest, to the stomach, and to the thighs that lightly resonate with the breathing movement. Lastly, we mentally go down to a point beneath our body and beneath our chair, a point that signifies the silence before all words, the point of inner listening.

Now we are all tasting the taste of inner silence, of quiet listening, of our inner depth. For a few moments all is intensely present within us and all around. Of course, the psychological mind has its own momentum and habits, and it cannot be completely neutralized. But a centering exercise is not designed to transform you. It is a glimpse and a reminder: "Look," it tells us, "this is your inner silence. Savor it, remember it in your heart."

For a while we savor the stillness with our eyes closed. Then, a minute or two later – not long enough to get tired and distracted – the facilitator's voice reaches our ears again. She invites us to start returning to the group, at our own pace, and open our eyes when we feel ready.

Moments from "Interpretive Reading"

Our minds focused and quiet, we turn to the philosophical text which the facilitator had prepared in advance. For this session she had chosen one page from the writings of the ancient Roman philosopher Marcus Aurelius, and the group now reads it in the procedure of "Interpretive reading": One after another we slowly read out loud the first paragraph over and over again. The repetitive reading creates a chant-like rhythm and prepares the mind for contemplation. We are encouraged to add brief interpretations as we read through the text, but no more than a few words so as to maintain the flow.

After three or four readings, we continue to the next paragraph. Our facilitator is always the first to read. She knows the text well, and she serves as a "tour guide" who takes us into it. She weaves in her reading brief comments here and there, or emphasizes certain words, and in this way turns our attention to important features in the text's landscape of ideas.

As we read through the text, we come to understand its main ideas. That is an obvious necessity – you cannot contemplate on a text you do not understand. But this is not a mere intellectual kind of understanding, because the exercise introduces in our mind important elements of contemplation: non-judgmental listening, resonating with the text, slowing down the mind through slow repetitive reading, and flowing with the "music" of the reading.

Our interpretive reading is, therefore, semi-contemplative – requiring silent inner listening to the ideas, but also some degree of discursive thinking. Our facilitator is experienced, and thanks to her precise and flowing facilitation, our minds grow in silence and depth as we go through the text.

When we reach the end of the page, after about thirty minutes, our minds are attuned to Marcus Aurelius' ideas and ready for deeper contemplative exercises.

Moments from "Ruminatio"

Several times during the session, between one round of interpretive reading and another, our facilitator conducts the exercise of "Ruminatio," also called "philosophical chanting." She selects one sentence from the paragraph we have just read, and we repeat it one after another in a predetermined order, over and over and over again, without interpretation and without interruption. The repetition creates a rhythm that dissolves the ordinary meaning of the words, so that they become a flow of sounds that silences all discursive thought. Fragments of ideas and images float in our minds, intimating nameless meanings like precious voices from elsewhere, reverberating within us with an intense presence.

Moments from "Precious speaking"

Now that the text's basic ideas are clear and alive in our minds, it is time to move on to the next stage and listen to them from our inner depth. To do so, the facilitator begins the exercise of "precious speaking."

In precious speaking we resonate with the text by giving voice to the insights that surface within us. We avoid expressing personal opinions or judgement, and instead listen "through" the text to the basic meanings that speak in it. A deep philosophical text expresses more than the writer's personal convictions if it is attuned to human life at large. What that philosopher had written on paper many years ago may express not just his individual thoughts but a greater realm of meanings.

Our facilitator leads us through several rounds of precious speaking. We give voice to the insights that appear within us, speaking concisely, limiting our speech to a few precise words, formulating each word as if it was a precious gem. This kind of speaking affects us profoundly: It focuses the mind and makes it attentive yet receptive. One by one we utter our poetic sentences in free order, creating an atmosphere of inwardness and breadth, as well as of group-togetherness.

What now speaks in our group is no longer personal ideas, but a choir of human voices that transcends any particular individual. We are giving voice to fundamental meanings that are embedded in life, to the ocean in which we always take part but are rarely fully aware of.

Voicing

After about an hour, the group has finished contemplating on specific ideas in the text. The facilitator now wants us to resonate with the text as a whole, and also to express our own voice in a more personal way. She wants us to resonate especially with one central concept in the text – Marcus Aurelius' notion of "the guiding principle" (which in his philosophy refers to the person's inner center of freedom and reason). For this purpose she starts the exercise called "Voicing."

"What does the 'guiding principle' do to me?" she asks us. But she does not want us to respond with opinions. Instead, she asks us to listen quietly within ourselves.

For a few moments we sit quietly and listen inwardly, our eyes either closed or hovering freely over the text. Then, when we are ready, we start writing gently, letting the writing flow from us and give voice to our inner depth. To the extent possible, we try making our sentences precise and condensed, even poetic.

Writing in a precise poetic style channels the minds into a gentle, focused attention to meanings and images. The gentle writing, as well as the inner search for precise words, intensify the sense of preciousness and realness. At times we feel as if we are writing what an inner voice is dictating to us. It is no wonder that the exercise of voicing is often the highlight of the session.

After we finish writing, we relax a little. We are tired from the long span of attention, and we know that the session is nearing its end. We examine what we have written – or perhaps what our inner depth has written – and we share it with the group by reading out our poetic-philosophical lines.

A precious moment

Earlier, halfway through the session, I experienced what we call a "precious moment." As our group was practicing interpretive reading, holding Marcus Aurelius' text in our hands, I felt it coming. I let go of my inner efforts and opened a quiet space of listening within me. I relaxed my mind and let my eyes glide over the lines. Gently I savored the words pronounced by my companions. They reverberated deep inside me, around me, and I let them speak without interfering.

All of a sudden a great presence enveloped me, vast and gentle, silent yet teeming with meanings. It kept emerging from the words of the text and dissolving my boundaries. Gone was the sharp border between inside-me and outside-me, between my own thought and external ideas. I was now part of a bigger immensity, a little wave in a great sea. I fell silent – waves do not speak about the ocean.

The words in the room were no longer merely ours – they belonged to a greater vastness. And the text was no longer merely by Marcus Aurelius, even though his fingers had written it on paper centuries ago. He only transcribed whatever had spoken in his mind. He was a philosopher, after all, and he had the greatness of mind to discern it and translate it into a human language.

Precious meanings echoed in me from the greater horizons, and I drank from them and quenched my yearning.

"What am I taking with me?"

As the session approaches its end, the intense atmosphere starts dissipating. Everybody is truly exhausted. It is time to relax, collect ourselves, and reflect on what has happened.

The facilitator announces the end of the contemplation, and asks us to take a few moments to look back and reflect on the entire session. After a minute or two of silence she speaks again. "Please share with us what you are taking with you from the session – an insight, an experience, an open question to think about…"

It is difficult to respond to such a question with precision. Contemplation is not designed to produce a bottom-line, a final statement. Like a musical concert, it is meaningful while it is happening, and when it ends it leaves you with no product to take home with you. Nevertheless, the attempt to give words to past moments helps to digest what had happened, and allows us to share our experiences with our companions.

One by one we speak briefly, while the others listen and nod or smile or reflect. When the round of sharing ends, the session is over, but for a few more moments we remain silent. Then we look at each other, smile, and wordlessly wave goodbye.

Chapter 3

REFLECTIONS ON THE MEANING OF DEEP PHILOSOPHY

Why Deep Philosophy?

"What can Deep Philosophy give me?" one might ask. "How can it satisfy my desires?"

A misleading assumption is hidden in this question: that something is valuable only if it satisfies an already-existing desire.

But philosophy does not have to satisfy existing desires in order to be valuable – it can also create new desires and needs and awaken dormant yearnings, ones that are higher than those you already feel. It can give birth to potential sensitivities that are still unborn, and cultivate new deeper understandings. In the process you might re-evaluate your old desires, and you might realize how trivial or insignificant they are, and might wish to transcend them.

A television addict might ask: "Who needs poems? Can they give me the excitement and diversion I get from watching TV every night? If not, what are they good for?"

A money-hungry businessman might ask: "Who needs Tolstoy or Plato? How much money can they get me? None? Well, then, why bother with them?"

How can we reply to such people? If they have never experienced a higher meaning of this kind, a theoretical explanation would not help.

The question is not, therefore, which desires Deep Philosophy satisfies, but which higher desires and yearnings it can create in us, which new sensitivities it can cultivate, which new "eyes" it can open. The question is, in short, which higher dimensions of human existence it can reveal.

One might wonder: What are those higher dimensions that Deep Philosophy promises to reveal?

But this cannot be explained to somebody who has never experienced them, except by vague metaphors, or circular explanations that explain nothing. How can you explain the meaning of poetry, or classical music, or philosophical contemplation to somebody who has never experienced any of it?

The proper response is: Come and practice with us, experience contemplation for yourself, and then you may see.

Deep philosophy produces nothing

What kind of results is Deep Philosophy supposed to produce?

None. Deep Philosophy is not designed to produce anything – not new theories or knowledge, not self-understanding, not peace or enjoyable experiences or novel skills. To be sure, some such results do indeed appear after contemplative sessions – inner silence, inspiring insights, heightened sensitivities – but these are byproducts, not the goal itself.

The practice of Deep Philosophy is akin to love: You kiss your beloved not in order to attain anything for yourself, but *out of* love. Likewise, you listen to music not to achieve anything, but out of your love for music. We practice Deep Philosophy out of love, yearning, wonder.

Today's world is governed by a pragmatic spirit that worships products that satisfy needs and desires. Deep Philosophy defies that trend. It does not seek to satisfy us but to awaken us to fundamental questions, to unsettle us, to raise marvel and longing.

For us, fundamental life-issues are not practical problems to be resolved, but fountains of life's inexhaustible meanings. They can never receive a final resolution. We therefore select for contemplation those special texts that present life-issues in their inexhaustible fullness, and through them we listen inwardly to the deep dimensions of human reality. One might say that we seek to cultivate our openness to those deeper dimensions – and that is generally true, as long as we do not interpret this as our final goal. A final goal, once formulated as a principle, tends to be petrified into a dead ideology. We simply keep contemplating to keep the wonder and yearning alive.

Performative Philosophy

"I participated in a Deep Philosophy session, and by the end of the session I hadn't gained any new knowledge!"

"Forget the end of the session – look at the session itself, all of it, moment by moment. Was it significant?"

Traditionally, philosophers philosophize in order reach some conclusion – a new theory, explanation, proof. At the end of their investigation they write their result on paper, and display it as an essay to be passed around from one reader to another.

But must philosophizing reach a conclusion in order to be of value?

When you go a lecture, you hope to return home with new knowledge, but when you go to a concert you don't expect to come back with something you had not possessed before. You listen carefully to the performance moment by moment, but despite the deeply significant experiences, when the lights are turned on, no conclusion remains in your possession. You go home empty-handed and yet enriched. Music is meaningful, like ballet or cinema, not because of what it produces, but because of what it is during the performance.

These can be called "performative activities." And likewise, there is also *performative philosophy*: This is a philosophical activity that is meaningful while it is happening. The philosophical moment itself is significant, even though it may not provide you with new philosophical assets to take home with you.

But why is Deep Philosophy a performative kind of philosophy? How come it does not produce an end-result – a new theory, an idea, a piece of knowledge?

Because what touches you in contemplation, as in the case of music, is not something you can capture in descriptions or theories. Theories are something you can take home with you, but the precious philosophical understandings that inspire you during a session cannot be preserved in sentences. They cannot be preserved at all – they live only in the moment.

The aspirations of Deep Philosophy

We practice philosophical contemplation because we seek the ground of existence. Philosophy, after all, is about the most fundamental issues of life and reality. We aspire to attain intimate communication with the foundation.

This is a tremendous mission, noble and inspiring, perhaps too presumptuous to be fully attainable by mere humans. Yet, human beings have been trying to accomplish it throughout history – by means of spiritual meditation, ritual and myth, music and prayer, and sometimes philosophy. Our way is philosophy, because we seek not just to feel but also to understand, not only to be touched but also to communicate. Through philosophical understandings we converse with the fundamental meanings of existence, or what we call "voices of reality."

Of course, we are always in reality, with or without Deep Philosophy. We are always waves in the ocean. But by philosophizing we make this relationship explicit, we let it speak in us and inspire us. Through our contemplation we manifest our encounter with reality, respond to it, elevate and enrich it.

As a mere individual, I cannot do this fully. I am always part of the historical discourse between humanity and reality. And just as I must rely on my English language (or whatever language I speak) to communicate with my neighbor, likewise I must rely on the "language" of the encounter between humanity and the foundation. Any intercourse which I might have with reality must occur within the context of the historical intercourse. I am always one small moment in a long historical love-story between humanity and the foundation.

That is why in Deep Philosophy we relate to the writings of previous philosophers. If we want to join humanity's encounter with reality, we must be historical. Historical texts of philosophy are part of the ongoing dialogue to which we wish to belong. If we want to dialogue with fundamental meanings, we must do so in the company of historical human voices.

The non-theory of Deep Philosophy

Deep Philosophy is not just a practice – it also has a network of theoretical ideas on the meaning of this practice. Yet, this network of ideas does not amount to a theory.

A theory is a coherent map about a given subject matter, whereas the ideas of Deep Philosophy are a multi-faceted network that is not assumed to be reducible to a unitary map.

Moreover, a theory of a practice is *about* the practice, separate from the practice and representing it from the outside, whereas the ideas of Deep Philosophy are part of the practice itself. They are used in our sessions as materials to practice with, as texts which contemplators contemplate upon and rewrite.

Therefore, while a theory is a fixed scheme, the ideas of Deep Philosophy are always in the process of being rewritten. Our "theoretical" ideas are the seeds which we cultivate by means of our contemplation, and from which our future practices will grow.

Furthermore, while a theory sets boundaries between the true and the false or the acceptable and unacceptable, the theoretical ideas of Deep Philosophy are voices to respond to and resonate with, not boundaries. They serve like musical phrases in an improvised jazz concert, which set the tone and key and rhythm, and invite you to respond with your own creativity. They do not give you a rule to follow, but a starting point to continue in accordance with the spirit that moves you.

Therefore, in Deep Philosophy we allow plurality and encourage it, both in our practice and in our reflections on it – not because we are tolerant, but because our human encounter with fundamental reality can be no less than a polyphony of the many human voices.

A philosophical theory as a door into a world

A philosophical theory is a network of ideas intended to represents (or "capture") some basic aspect of our world. But for us, a philosophical theory, if it is deep, is more than an abstract representation or an intellectual object. It expresses a world of fundamental meanings. And importantly, it enables us to enter it.

We humans have a marvelous capacity to enter alternate worlds. When we read a novel, we enter in our minds the fictional world which it describes. We identify ourselves with some characters, we love some of them and feel happy for their fortunes and sad for their misfortunes, we feel fear or hope according to the events, as if we were living in that world. To be sure, we are never absorbed in that world completely, and we never forget that the novel is a fiction and that we are sitting in our armchair with a book in our hands. Nevertheless, we enter the world of the novel to some extent, in some part of our mind so to speak.

In a similar manner, we can enter the world of a movie, or the world of a monopoly game, and feel strong emotions connected with the events that happen in them as if they were really happening to us.

Something similar happens in text-contemplation when we enter a philosophical world – the world portrayed by the text – and explore it from the inside. We do not just think "about" it, but rather make it present to us and enter it. Yet, there is an important difference here. Unlike the world of a novel or a movie, the world we enter in philosophical contemplation is not composed of particular things – objects, people, cities, events, etc. – but of general ideas, or concepts, or more precisely meanings. If the text we contemplate is truly philosophical, then the reality it portrays is composed of fundamental meanings, or what we call "voices of reality."

For this to happen, we must maintain the appropriate state of mind and attitude. We must not focus on the ideas of the text as ideas, but "look through" them to the world of meanings they express. When we do so, the philosophical text acts as a door through which we enter a fundamental reality and immerse ourselves in it, like a wave in an ocean.

Texts for contemplation

Not all philosophical texts are equally suitable for contemplation. For the purpose of contemplation a text must be deep, in the sense that it points beyond the surface of definable ideas, and thus cannot be captured in a summary or exhausted by a description. As much as we delve in it, it keeps revealing new facets, pointing to further depths of meaning.

Even if the text is suitable for contemplation, it may or may not reveal its depth to us, depending on our attitude and state of mind. We are not likely to discover its depth if we try to analyze it intellectually, as external observers. We must enter the world of the text and relate to it from the inside, changing our normal mental state to inner listening, which is what we do in contemplation.

But not every text allows us to relate to it through inner listening. If a texts describes a world of objects, then it forces me to remain an external observer – I cannot think about an object from the inside. Thus, texts that are too objective or factual, that are analyzable into definite bits of concepts or information, are not suitable for contemplation. For contemplation, a text must present us with a new world-order, not governed by the usual structure of subject and object, observer and observed, thinker and ideas. Entering such a text means entering a world in which I am no longer a psychological subject who thinks "about" things. And now I am transformed into a wave in the ocean.

The polyphony of philosophical writings

All philosophical writings interest us in Deep Philosophy, as long as they relate to the depth of life. We have little interest in intellectual exercises that forgot their root in living reality, even if they are considered philosophical.

What we seek in a text is depth, not factual correctness. And depth is primarily a matter of where the text is coming from – its roots in the fundamental meanings of human reality, and the testimony it gives to those inexhaustible, generative meanings. For us, the source of a text is of greater importance than what it is about, or what it says about it.

Thus, when we contemplate on a text, we do not agree or disagree with it, we do not judge it for rightness or wrongness. We accept deep texts as testimonies of human life – just as a song is a testimony of the musician who composed it or who sings it. We accept them as expressions – some clearer and some opaque, some more direct and powerful and others less so – of the rich polyphony of voices of human reality.

These voices of the depth, so to speak, may be different in different philosophical writings, but even so they are not contradictory. They are like different sounds arising from the same forest: the whistle of the wind through the tall and short treetops, the murmur of the large leafy leaves and the rustle of the small dry leaves, the creaking of the tree-trunks, the thump of the branches as they fall to the ground. The forest is not limited to one sound. Like the polyphony of the forest, so is the polyphony of philosophical voices, which is to say – of human reality. There is room for all of them side by side, and together they enrich one another.

In Deep Philosophy we seek to make present those fundamental voices that speak in deep philosophical texts, and that are at the basis of anything meaningful in human reality. We aim to participate in this tremendous polyphonic concert and be part of it.

The power of philosophizing

Many philosophers throughout history tell us that philosophy can transform us. Thus, philosophizing for Plato takes us out of the cave in which we are imprisoned. For the Stoic philosophers, philosophizing helps awaken our true self – the "guiding principle" that guides us in the ways of reason, inner freedom, equanimity, and harmony with the cosmos. For Spinoza, philosophizing leads to the quiet wisdom that is the intellectual love of all (or God). Nietzsche's poetic philosophy inspires us to overcome our small self. Bergson's philosophy teaches us to note the holistic qualities of our consciousness that normally escape us. And the list goes on.

This might seem strange. Philosophy is typically viewed as the study of abstract universal ideas that are far removed from everyday concerns. How can it influence our concrete life?

The history of philosophy reveals at least two ways to do so. One is the way of applied philosophy: The philosopher discusses the issues at hand in the abstract, reaches some conclusion in the abstract, and then applies it to concrete situations. Philosophizing, then, remains an abstract investigation, conducted intellectually in the philosopher's study. Only after the investigation has ended is its final conclusion exported to life.

The second way is more direct: Philosophizing can impact us while it is happening, because the philosophical activity itself, not just its end-result, can inspire us. It has the power to awaken our inner sensitivities and open us to deeper dimensions of life. Indeed, various philosophies throughout the ages developed practical ways to activate this power: The Stoic imagination exercises, Neoplatonic meditations, the poetic writing of Romantic philosophers, and the like.

Deep Philosophy too takes the second way. In Deep Philosophy, exploring philosophical ideas is part of the contemplative process. Philosophizing impacts us because contemplation impacts us, since the two are fused into one movement. Through our contemplative exercises, ideas act in our inner depth, inspiring us and changing us.

Chapter 4

EXPERIENTIAL UNDERSTANDING

Philosophical contemplation, the central activity of Deep Philosophy, is a form of philosophy that is both intellectual and experiential. On the one hand, through contemplation we receive understandings of life or ourselves, but on the other hand these understandings involve profound experiences, often in the form of a powerful sense of preciousness and realness. In fact, in deep moments of contemplation there is no clear distinction between the element of experiencing and the element of understanding, and the two are merged together.

One may call the result "experiential understanding," and it includes several typical kinds of experiences.

The experience of precious insights

When we contemplate on a philosophical text, whether in an organized exercise or unintentionally when we happen to read the text gently and attentively, we may suddenly notice a quiet presence encompassing us. As we continue savoring the words, we may find that nameless insights flutter in our minds, accompanied by a sense of preciousness. We may not have the words to describe what is happening to us, but we unmistakably sense it as profoundly meaningful.

This state of mind is familiar to practitioners of text contemplation in several spiritual traditions around the world.

Common to them is the observation that the reading of a text with a special kind of attentive state of mind may elicit meaningful insights. The Christian *Lectio Divina*, a structured technique of reading Christian scriptures, is one such example.

Traditionally, these experiences are given religious interpretations – "I heard the Word of God," "The Holy Spirit spoke in me," etc. But putting aside those religious speculations, the basic idea is straightforward: A silent attentive reading of deep texts can produce new understandings, difficult to articulate in words yet profoundly meaningful.

When this happens to us, we realize that we are witnessing something of special significance. We are not merely having a good feeling or interesting thoughts, but discerning something of importance that inspires us, awakens us, and elevates us.

Such deep experiential understandings intimate to us the existence of a dimension of our being that is usually inactive and dormant, or what we call inner depth. And once we experience it awakening – not necessarily in an overwhelming way, sometimes very subtly – we realize that there are aspects of life with which we are normally not in touch. Something exceedingly precious hides underneath the surface of our everyday life, and yet it is within reach. We wish to experience it again, to explore it, to witness the new horizons it opens. This is an urge to keep practicing Deep Philosophy.

The bubble experience

As Deep Philosophers, we seek precious understandings even beyond the limited time of contemplation sessions. Indeed, in the midst of our normal everyday activity, we sometime notice within us a spontaneous "bubble" of understanding rising from our inner depth, precious and meaningful.

This happens to most of us, although most people do not typically pay much attention to it. The experience is not necessarily dramatic – it may be hardly noticeable, but it is somehow different, and we might savor it with some degree of marvel. If we notice it, we might sense that we have received a little gem of understanding.

I say "we have received" because we experience it not as a result of our own active thinking but as an uninvited arrival. The little new understanding materializes in our awareness unexpectedly as if from elsewhere. We feel that some hidden source within us, beyond our familiar thinking patterns, beyond the realm of our familiar mind, has given birth to this new understanding. We call it "a bubble of understanding," or a "bubble" for short, because it behaves like the tiny bubbles of air rising from the obscure depths of a lake to the face of the water.

It is not easy to say much about such bubbles, because they are very difficult to translate into words. When we do try to describe them, our descriptions seem to miss the essence. To give an example from my own experience, I might say: "The grasshopper turned towards me, and I was suddenly struck by the realization that both of us, that insect and me, belong to the same river of life" – but these words sound like a cliché. They do not capture the sense of marvel that I experienced and the preciousness of the insight. Something of value had been received, but once I tried to translate it into words it evaporated.

Anybody who remembers experiencing such bubbles knows that their significance or preciousness cannot be captured by the words used to articulate them. Evidently, what is precious and meaningful in a bubble is not merely its intellectual content, but also how, and where, and from where within us it came. An ineffable dimension of our being has spoken, one that is not translatable into ordinary thoughts.

Some might be tempted to interpret their bubble as if it was "given" to them by some alien intelligence or a higher being, especially if one is inclined to religious or metaphysical conjectures. But we do not need to indulge in speculations about the source of this experience. The point here is much more modest: The bubble experience teaches us that there are aspects of our being that are usually dormant, and that awaken only in rare moments. Evidently, there are sources of experiential understanding within us that go beyond intellectual thinking.

Ideas from elsewhere

It is often assumed that thoughts are all alike – just thoughts. Presumably, they are all born in our mind in essentially the same way, by the same thinking faculty, whatever it is. But if we carefully attend to our thinking, to the qualities of our thoughts as they appear in our mind, we discover that they are not all the same.

"Bubbles" of insights teach us an important distinction between thoughts which we experience as being produced by us, and thoughts which we experience as entering our minds from beyond the sovereignty of the self.

Thoughts of the first type are so common that we hardly ever bother to think about them. They include thoughts produced by our deliberate effort to think, but also thoughts that we think absent-mindedly, thoughts that are at the center of attention and those that are part of the background chatter that normally hums in the mind. None of these thoughts surprises us – we say without difficulty that such a thought is *my* thought and that it is I myself who produced it. This "mine-ness" is somewhat analogous to the way I experience my hand movements, both those I make deliberately and those I make unthinkingly. I experience them both as my own actions, as opposed to an involuntary twitch which I experience as forced upon me by my body.

In contrast, in special moments a thought materializes in my mind as if from elsewhere. An obvious example is a "bubble" that appears in my mind unexpectedly, as described earlier. But this is not the only example. Another example is that of inspired writing, when the words formulate themselves in the writer's mind as if by themselves, sometimes even forcing themselves upon the mind and flooding it. Such experiences are not the same as unexpected one-time bubbles of insight, but they point to the same conclusion: Some of our ideas emerge from an unusual dimension of our being that is different from the source of ordinary thinking. Unlike ordinary thoughts, they are not under the control of the self, but unlike obsessive thoughts they do not impose themselves on us by force. On the contrary, they inject into us a sense of preciousness, freedom and plenitude.

What is this hidden fountain of ideas within us? Whatever it is, we call it our "inner depth." Although this is a metaphor, it is not an arbitrary one. It is analogous to the hidden roots that hide in the depth of the earth and produce flowers and trees, and to the underground springs in the belly of the earth that bring water to the surface.

The experience of realness

An important experience in philosophical contemplation is the sense of heightened realness. When we contemplate on a text and quietly listen inwardly, we sometimes sense that everything within us and even around us attains a powerful realness, much greater than usual: our thoughts, our feelings, our bodily awareness, our experience of the surroundings.

It is difficult to explain this to somebody who has never noticed such an experience. In our daily life, all our experiences feel equally real. The realness of a taste in my mouth is the same as the realness of a melody in my ears, and my headache is just as real as my itch. Indeed, it seems to make no sense to ask which of these two is "more real." Although one of them might be more intense than the other, it certainly does not have a greater realness. In our daily life, realness does not come in degrees.

But in fact, the sense of greater realness does appear in special moments. Mystics report experiencing a tremendous reality that dwarfs or overpowers their own being, and philosophers of religion such as Rudolf Otto and William James describe it as an important element in religious experiences. Likewise, in precious moments in nature we may feel the vastness of nature and sense a powerful stillness invading our inner being, making everything brimming with realness.

Something similar happens in deep contemplative moments, when we feel submerged in a powerful realness enveloping us. However, unlike many religious or nature experiences, contemplative experiences also involve understanding, not just feeling. At the height of contemplation on a philosophical text, the thoughts and insights in our mind may be infused with a powerful realness, as if their meanings have a special weight, so to speak, and their reality is greater than that of mere abstract ideas.

We need not interpret these experiences literally, as manifesting metaphysical realities, but it is also important not to ignore their special quality or dismiss them. They indicate that something special is happening within us during those moments, and that a dormant aspect of our being is being activated and revealed.

The experience of inner depth, preciousness, plenitude

The sense of realness is typically accompanied by other experiences such as the experience of inner depth, of preciousness, and of plenitude.

We have the experience of inner depth when we sense that a hidden aspect of our being is awakening within us and unifying our entire being. We then feel as if we are in touch with our own source. Gone is our usual fragmentation, and a concentrated center now unifies us, more primordial – so it feels – than the multiplicity of our mental chatter, feelings and actions. This inner center was familiar to ancient Hellenistic philosophers of the Stoic school. They called it "the guiding principle" and regarded it as the true center of our being that guides us in wisdom and harmony with the cosmos.

The experience of inner depth is often accompanied by a sense of preciousness, which is quite common in philosophical contemplation. In such moments we feel that our insights and experiences are of special value and perfection. It is as if we are submerged in a precious gem, in a sphere of precious harmony, where everything is just right.

The sense of inner depth and of preciousness are also associated with the experience of plenitude. Here we sense that we are animated by a fountain of creative energy that is giving birth to rich insights and understandings. New ideas surface in our minds from an unknown source, profound and surprising, and we can only receive them and let them act in us.

These different experiences are often mingled with each other, and the distinction between them is somewhat arbitrary.

The experience of a polyphony of meanings

Normally, when we read a text containing statements or theories – a newspaper report, a journal article, a political analysis – our immediate inclination is to assess it and judge it as true or false, or at least as probable or improbable. We accept it or doubt it or reject it, we agree with it or disagree, and even when we suspend judgement we reserve the right to judge it in the future.

But something very different happens when we contemplate on a philosophical text. We listen to it attentively without judging it, as when we listen to poetry or music. We are captivated by the flow of ideas, by their meaning and depth, without judging them as true or false. We then sense a polyphonic music of meanings floating in our mind.

This may seem peculiar. How can you possibly reflect on a philosophical text or idea in disconnection from the question of whether it is acceptable or inacceptable? After all, it makes statements about reality that must be either true or false. Its original purpose is to declare that that's the way things are.

Evidently, in contemplation we do not treat a philosophical text as a statement about the world. We do not regard it as an attempt to portray what reality is like, and we do not attend to the correspondence between the text and the world. We attend, rather, to the way the text acts in us, to the flow of ideas it elicits into us, and how they resonate with our personal life-experience.

But this requires a special kind of inner attitude. Because we can experience a text as a polyphony of meanings only if we hold back our tendency to judge, and instead savor its words and ideas as they flow in our mind. This is the role of the various techniques of text contemplation.

The value of contemplative experiences

The contemplation of philosophical ideas is colored by experiential qualities that we sense as deeply meaningful and rewarding. Nevertheless, we pursue these experiences not because they feel good, but because through them we encounter the greater reality which we seek. Here the analogy with love is instructive: Lovers might enjoy the experience of love, but that is not why they seek the presence of their beloved. If you are truly in love, you are in love with your beloved, not with your feelings. Conversely, if all you care about is the sweetness of your own feelings, then your love is not true love. Likewise, in Deep Philosophy we contemplate because we yearn to encounter our beloved – the foundation of reality in its realness.

This desire to get in touch with the real is a universal human motivation that is found in religion, science, poetry and art, as well as in mainstream philosophy. Yet, there is something special in contemplative philosophy that distinguishes it from many of the others: It seeks the foundation of reality not just experientially and not just intellectually, but with both of these dimensions intertwined together, through experiential understanding.

Chapter 5

REVERIES ON THE BROADER HORIZONS

Let me now speculate a little bit on the broader meaning of philosophical contemplation – not because I have great truths to declare, but as additional harmonies to our music of ideas, to enrich our understanding of Deep Philosophy. I don't claim these speculations to be literally true – matters of depth cannot be captured with theories. These are voices in our polyphonic understanding, and we can listen to them just as contemplators attend to a text, beyond agreement and disagreement.

Philosophical madness

We sit together and contemplate on a text – a philosophy text. Not poetry, not literature, not history or world affairs, but philosophy. Why?

Because we seek the deepest roots of our being, and philosophy is about the foundation. It is not about this particular woman or that particular event, it is not limited to this city or that island – it is about the most basic and universal of all. Philosophers seek the most fundamental.

The foundation is what mainstream philosophers have been exploring for ages, trying to capture it in their theories. But for us in Deep Philosophy, a theory is too abstract and too remote. We are in love, sick with the Platonic Eros for that which is real, and theories of the beloved would not quench our thirst. We want reality to swell within us and speak in our inner depth. "Inner depth" is the name of the place where reality touches us with its fundamental meanings.

Some might dismiss us as dreamers. It is a folly to dream of touching reality, they might say, even a form of madness. And perhaps they are right. But better be mad dreamers than cold professional thinkers who satisfy themselves with lukewarm logical games. Because through our passionate folly we are truly real, and through our dreams of realness we reach realness. Yearnings can be deeper and more far-reaching than careful abstractions.

Ours is a philosophical sort of mad longing. Philosophical – because we use philosophical theories to reach out to the depth, even though we seek to go beyond philosophy, to the fundamental voices that live before all theories. Our contemplation is intended to carry us towards the foundation as far as humanly possible, or as far as our personal capacities would allow.

With the modesty of those who know they are mad we say: Deep Philosophy aims at the depths that extend beyond philosophy. By contemplating on philosophical texts we reach out beyond all texts.

Philosophical reverence

I contemplate on a fundamental idea and vacate myself, letting a deep understanding unravel itself within me. This is a philosophical act, because it turns me towards the foundation. It is also an act of depth, because it reaches down towards the depths. That deep understanding may use the intellect to formulate words for it, but it does not belong to the intellect. It belongs to the depth.

Depth is never my own depth. It is not something I possess or control – it belongs to greater horizons. That is why a genuine act of deep philosophizing is precious, even sacred, because it embodies an understanding whose roots reach out far beyond me. Through it, I stand in the presence of an encompassing reality.

But the act of deep philosophizing also receives its preciousness from another source: from the yearning to reach out beyond oneself and be part of greater horizons. The philosopher himself may not know it, but if he is engaged in a genuine act of deep philosophizing, then he is transcending his individual boundaries in an act of reverence in the face of the great ocean.

A genuine act of deep philosophizing is, one might say, like a prayer without a god as its target. It does not matter whether or not you believe in prayer – the point is your inner attitude, not your retroactive interpretation of what you were doing.

Philosophical testimonies

In one sense, each historical text of philosophy was composed at a certain time in history by a certain individual person – texts do not appear in the world by themselves. But in another sense, what writers put on paper was born out of a realm broader than their little individual selves. After all, one does not invent one's life – one finds oneself already embedded in it. A text, therefore, can sometimes express a broader range of voices than the writer's thoughts.

Most texts, of course, are mere products of psychological forces, of the writers' feelings or thinking mechanisms and the blind impact of their particular environment. Such are many newspaper articles, novels and romances, even standard philosophy essays – most of them are not deep enough to resonate with the depths of human reality.

But some philosophical texts are special – they have a unique potential. Philosophy is about the fundamental dimensions of our world. So if a philosopher manages to write his text *from* the foundation he is writing about, if he is able to write about it by resonating with it, then he may be giving voice to the great ocean – more so or less so, depending on his skills and sensitivities.

When a wave resonates with the motions of the ocean, its local resonance is a testimony to those greater movements. And if that wave could write, its words would be a testimony to the ocean. Hence, some philosophy texts are testimonies to the ocean of fundamental reality, if one reads them as testimonies. They carry the sounds of its currents, if one knows how to listen.

But of course, not every philosophical text is like that. Many are no more than intellectual acrobatics. Even then, however, one sometimes finds among the many pages a few paragraphs of testimony to something greater. And then, if one knows how to read them, one can listen to the sounds of the ocean.

That is how, in Deep Philosophy, we find our texts for contemplation: We search through piles of philosophical writings, hoping to find a handful of precious gems – a couple of pages here, a chapter there – that would testify to the human resonance with the ocean of reality.

Realness is indispensable

One might ask us: "What is this fundamental reality which you, Deep Philosophers, are after? And how can you tell when you have found it, or when you are getting nearer?"

Honesty dictates that we should hesitate here. Any talk of "fundamental reality" might sound too pompous. Even though we mean these words in a qualified human sense – in the sense of "reality as far as it is accessible to humans" – they still sound pretentious. Even though we limit ourselves to the foundation of *human* reality, any talk of the foundation should be treated with healthy suspicion.

But let us not talk of reality as an independent thing lying somewhere and waiting to be found. Let us not think of it as an object of our thoughts and theories. The reality to which I testify is already manifested within me. It is not a thing outside me and not a subjective feeling inside me, because it encompasses both inside and outside. Reality, after all, is the root of everything, residing everywhere, in me as well as out there. That is why in special moments, when it manifests itself in me, it appears as a presence everywhere, as the preciousness of all, as the realness of the reality of which I am a part.

And if this talk of "realness" still sounds to you too embarrassing, then let me say that I cannot afford to discard it without losing my soul. I cannot dismiss my yearning for reality or my sense of realness as if it was a fiction; I cannot treat the age-old human search for truth as if it was a mere illusion. It shapes who I am.

The voices beyond the text

I sit in contemplation and contemplate on a philosophical text. The topic of the text may be some theory of love or freedom or beauty or whatever, but the topic of the contemplative act itself is deeper – it is the human reality that has given birth to these abstract ideas. The ideas themselves are relevant too, but as an intermediary medium: They direct me beyond themselves to the fundamental meanings that are at their roots. Ideas are objects of the intellect formulated in words, but fundamental meanings are voices of reality itself – they are more primordial than words, concepts or theories.

Thus, the contemplative act is composed of two elements mixed together: first, the grasping of the philosophical ideas, and second, from these ideas to the fundamental meanings beyond them.

The first step is about ideas: Intellectual units for the mind to grasp and manipulate and apply, and transmit from person to person in speech or in writing. But such intellectual units still lack grounding in human reality. They may have semantic meanings, but they do not yet have meaningfulness. They may describe or represent certain objective facts, but they are not yet embedded in the ocean that gives life to life. Meaningfulness, as in the case of plenitude or preciousness, is not a thing to describe – certainly not from the outside – but something to receive and live from. Thus, philosophical ideas – if they have any depth, if they are more than intellectual constructs – are testimonies to the original meanings before being objectified into ideas and structured for the mind to grasp.

We contemplate on a text because we cannot reach out to fundamental meanings directly. We cannot place them in our mind as we do with a concept or sentence, because they are not mental objects at all. But through the text, if the contemplation is successful, their presence will be embodied within us.

Understanding by participating

As philosophers of the depth, we seek the fundamental meanings we call "voices of reality." And since we cannot capture them in our theories, we sing along with them to take part in their polyphonic orchestra.

"Taking part" is our way to understand the music of fundamental meanings. What you cannot objectify into an object of thought, what you cannot think-about, you may still be able to sing with. The violin understand the flute by playing along with it and accompanying it meaningfully. You can play with the orchestra to understand it, at least as do listeners in the audience who hum the melody in their hearts.

The wave does not inspect the ocean from the outside. It embodies the ocean's movements and lets them resonates within, and thus gives voice to the primordial water.

The sense of realness

From the perspective of the tedious everyday moment, realness might seem barely noticeable. The chair over there is real, my coughing is real, your smile is real, the street noise is real, are they not? Real is real, and there is little of interest to say about it – so it seems.

Only in moments of special realness do I discover how real realness can be, how majestic and precious. Because suddenly all is real like it has rarely been before, present with gentle intensity, brimming with silence, and I too am part of it. Yet, nothing in my world has changed: All facts and objects are precisely what they had been before – the same colors, the same shapes and angles – only more real.

What is this realness? That is not something to define but to witness. Realness is not an object of thought and description, nor a content of the mind to grasp – that is why realness does not change the objects I perceive around me. Nor is it an emotion; on the contrary, all emotions are silenced in those moments. Realness encompasses me, engulfing both subject and object, thinker and thought, mind and its contents.

Such moments may appear spontaneously, sometimes in silent walks in nature, sometimes while listening to sublime music, or even in the midst of a busy day. But when they take place in text-contemplation, they are more than mere realness – they are also pregnant with meaning. Contemplation manifests primordial meanings in utter realness.

More than just psychology

Do I dare to claim that I can contemplate on the ocean of reality? I am a mere human being, a speck in the universe, trapped in my minuscule human psychology.

Yet, I am not completely trapped in my smallness. I am attuned to broader horizons beyond my narrow boundaries. And through this attunement, greater realities manifest themselves within me, just as the great wind manifests itself in the field through the trembling little flowers.

I am not just a psychological mechanism, because my inner depth is open to vast realms. And thanks to this openness I can contemplate: I let go of the opinions I possess in my psychology, I quiet down my automatic thinking, and silently I listen deep within. Now I am attuned to the voices of reality, and I resonate with them just as the little flower resonates with the breeze that blows around it.

Part B

ROOTS OF DEEP PHILOSOPHY

Any philosophical endeavor that seeks to explore the foundation of human existence, such as Deep Philosophy, is part of a longer history of ideas, both personal and cultural, which started before its birth. It emerged at a specific point in time in the lives of individual thinkers, and at a certain point in history.

This suggests that understanding the historical roots of a philosophical approach such as ours can provide a fuller understanding of it. Admittedly, sometimes the historical roots may be ignored for practical purposes, especially in the case of philosophies that are highly technical and abstract. To a large extent they can be viewed as relatively independent systems of thought that can be understood quite independently of their history.

However, a non-historical viewpoint is less appropriate in the case of philosophical approaches that seek to explore concrete life as it is lived. Such approaches often reflect specific personal and cultural experiences, assumptions, yearnings and predicaments, which have to be appreciated to achieve a full understanding of the philosophy in question. This viewpoint is even less appropriate in the case of Deep Philosophy, which involves a personal dialogue between the individual philosophical practitioner and life. Such a dialogue is always embedded in a specific personal and historical context and colored by it.

Furthermore, Deep Philosophy is historical by its very nature: When we contemplate on historical texts we are in dialogue with historical thinkers. Our attempt to relate to the foundation of our existence through voices from the past makes Deep Philosophy part of a longer human dialogue with reality.

Chapter 6

THE DEEP PHILOSOPHY GROUP

Deep Philosophy was founded by a small international group of people who call themselves the Deep Philosophy Group. To understand the nature of Deep Philosophy, we must follow their work and see how their explorations and visions have shaped it. Naturally, I can account for my own experiences much better than for those of my companions. Although I am reluctant to talk about my personal life, it seems to me that sharing some personal experiences would help to shed light on the history of the Deep Philosophy Group.

Early aspirations

Like many young students, I entered university with a vague aspiration to learn about the meaning of human existence. I decided to double-major in philosophy and psychology, and in the first few years I encountered many stimulating ideas. Yet, like many other students I soon started feeling a disturbing ambivalence, which would accompany me for many years. On the one hand, I was fascinated by philosophy's attempt to address the big issues of life: What can we hope to know about the world? What is the mind and what is consciousness? What is true love? What does it mean to be free or authentic? On the other hand, the philosophical ideas I encountered seemed too abstract and remote: I felt that they did not really touch the living human experience and did not shed light on real life. They appeared to be not about life, but about an impoverished abstraction of life that lacked concrete reality.

Some students who experience a similar frustration end up leaving philosophy for other disciplines. I persevered because despite my dissatisfaction, I still hoped to find a kind of philosophy that would be personally meaningful. Always vacillating between hope and disillusion, I completed my doctoral studies in the USA and started teaching philosophy at a university. I worked in the area of philosophy of psychology, publishing professional articles and participating in conferences, but throughout these years my thirst for a more meaningful philosophy continued to torment me.

I came to see a split between life and philosophy: Concrete life offers us rich and deep experiences – in nature, in friendship and love, at work, in literature and music and art. Philosophy, in contrast, offers us intellectual reflections and theories. Why can't the two be combined into one unified movement? Must we choose between experiencing life and understanding it? I wanted both combined. I yearned to touch life with a living form of wisdom.

In the early 1990s, while teaching at a university in Texas, I heard about "philosophical counseling" – a new practice that had begun a decade earlier in Europe and was practiced by two small groups, one in Germany and one in Holland. Its impact on the general public was negligible at the time, but when I heard that its vision was to make philosophy relevant to ordinary people, my interest was aroused. Eagerly I traveled twice to Europe and met people from both groups. Although I soon realized that they were still making their first experimental steps, I sympathized with their ambitions.

Their main format of activity was that of individual counseling: one-on-one meetings between a philosophical counselor and a client. The philosophical counselor, like an ordinary psychological counselor, would meet a client for a series of sessions, and the two would converse about the client's personal predicaments and issues. To distinguish themselves from psychologists, those early philosophical practitioners tried to develop a counseling dialogue that would be philosophical in nature, although I was not convinced that they had succeeded. For one thing, their counseling seemed to deal primarily with the client's personal problems, just like in psychotherapy, and not with the fundamental life-issues that characterize philosophical discourse.

With some doubts in mind, I decided to join this endeavor and try to develop a philosophical counseling that would be truly philosophical, and would establish the meeting point I had been hoping to find between philosophical discourse and concrete human existence.

I embarked upon this endeavor with much energy and started developing my own version of philosophical counseling, at first experimentally with volunteers, and later with paying clients. My clients' reactions were positive, although it was hard to tell whether this was because of the allegedly philosophical content of my counseling. After a while I consolidated my conception of philosophical counseling, I published articles about it and gave lectures and presentations. I also envisioned and co-organized the First International Conference on Philosophical Counseling, which took place in 1994 at the University of British Columbia in Canada. Soon afterwards, the idea of philosophical practice (or counseling) started spreading, and new groups of philosophical practice emerged in several countries in Europe and North America. I began teaching a new course of philosophical counseling at the University of Haifa in Israel. Additional publications and activities by fellow philosophical practitioners started to appear.

But despite these developments, I became more and more disillusioned, and I started distancing myself from my past work. I was concerned that philosophical counseling (or "philosophical practice" as it now came to be called) was intellectual and remote, very much like academic philosophy. Analyzing with clients their personal experiences is still treating life intellectually.

Worse, I started questioning whether this kind of counseling was philosophical at all. Philosophizing, as it has been practiced in the West for more than 2600 years, means exploring general life-issues, not discussing the specific personal problem of a specific individual. It means seeking to understand fundamental issues of life and reality, not analyzing Mary's problems at work or Peter's fights with his wife.

While continuing to search for better ways to make my counseling truly philosophical and yet concretely personal, I came to realize the value of using traditional philosophical writings in my work with people. Brief philosophical texts from the past can serve as rich sources of wisdom for self-understanding, provided they are used not as an authority to follow, but as raw materials to develop into personal understandings. Using philosophical texts seemed to be a good step towards connecting my practice to the spirit of philosophy. After all, philosophy is a historical discourse in which thinkers respond to each other and to previous thinkers. You cannot seriously do philosophy, in the Western sense of the term, without relating to relevant philosophers of the past as if they had never existed. You cannot invent philosophical thought from nothing.

And so, in my counseling with individuals I would often give my counselees brief texts as potential starting points for self-investigation. I also started working with groups, and developed a format of philosophical self-reflection groups in which participants used traditional philosophical ideas as tools for examining their personal lives and experiences. The participants would share with each other relevant experiences and insights while aiming at a deeper self-understanding.

At the same time, in my writings and lectures I kept calling upon my fellow philosophical practitioners to search for more deeply philosophical directions. As opposed to the common tendency at the time, I suggested that philosophical practitioners should work not with people who want to solve personal problems – these can go see a psychologist – but with those who yearn to enrich their lives and elevate it. Many traditional philosophers throughout the ages believed that philosophy could lead to self-development – why not follow their vision? Why imitate psychology with its problem-solving focus? Philosophy's goal has never been to normalize people, in other words to take them back to normal life, but on the contrary, to awaken them from their "normal" slumber.

Given my prominent position in the movement, I had the opportunity to voice my concerns on many occasions. Many read my articles or heard me speak, yet their responses were no more than guarded interest. The main reason was, I now believe, that there were no alternatives on the table. Counseling is an already-familiar format of activity, known from psychology, and it is easy to copy it. But how do you start a completely new kind of philosophizing that would yield deep and meaningful personal understandings?

First experiments with philosophical contemplation

I cannot overstate how frustrating all of this was to me in the late 1990s and early 2000s. I felt that I had reached a dead-end in my search for a life-giving form of philosophy. Was it possible that philosophy was destined to remain divorced from life, and to do nothing more than intellectualizing in the abstract?

But a new source of inspiration came to my aid, at first as an unrelated activity, and later profoundly reshaping my philosophical work. In the early 1990s, while still teaching philosophy full time at a university, I visited a contemplative monastery, and I was immediately captivated by the contemplative spirit. Although I never came to believe in the monks' Catholic faith, nor in any other institutional religion, I was deeply moved by the monks' spiritual life and spiritual practices. Thanks to the monks' generous hospitality, I started spending weeks and months at a time in this monastery. During those years I gained experience in contemplative techniques and other spiritual practices. I was fortunate to receive several profound spiritual experiences that shook me to the core and influenced me deeply. Yet, since I had always been suspicious of dogmatic beliefs, whether religious or other, I remained a free-spirited spiritual seeker.

It was only several years later, in the early 2000's, that the idea started taking shape in my mind to combine the philosophical quest with spiritual practices into a contemplative kind of philosophy. Why not philosophize about basic life-issues using contemplative techniques? If those techniques work with religious texts in which I did not believe, why couldn't they be adapted to philosophical texts too?

My first experiments were with the technique of text-contemplation called *"Lectio Divina,"* which I had learned at the monastery. In this technique, the contemplator reads silently a few sentences from a text while listening inwardly, and then continues through several steps to a deeper state of mind. This practice can be structured in a number of ways, but my experiments gradually gave birth to a version that I found appropriate for philosophical contemplation. Instead of religious texts, I used brief excerpts, profound and condensed, from larger philosophical essays, and I was delighted to discover that they too touched me deeply and elevated me. In contrast to religious contemplation which is based on the belief in religious dogmas and scriptures, I found that it was important to listen to the philosophical text without agreeing or disagreeing with it, treating it as a precious voice among many others voices of human reality. After a while I started using additional contemplative techniques, such as spiritual writing and spiritual walks in silence.

Towards the mid-2000s I started feeling that I was ready to share my practices with others, and I began facilitating contemplative group activities. Not all my experiments were successful, but as I continued working with small groups of colleagues and ex-students, my practices gradually consolidated. Little by little my philosophical-contemplative practice gained focus and structure and started bearing fruit.

Online companionships

My next step was the transition to long-term groups that would work together for several weeks. Since I wanted to work with international groups, it was necessary to meet on a video-chat platform such as Skype.

Thanks to my acquaintance with many philosophical practitioners, I could reach out to them and invite them to participate in experimental online sessions. In each session we used a selected philosophical text, and we contemplated on it for about an hour. I learned that a good contemplation session requires a clear and focused structure. The mind must be allowed to fully concentrate on the text and silently listen to it internally. Complicated exercises, discussions and deliberations are too distracting.

At first I shared the role of facilitation with the handful of colleagues who had joined me, each one facilitating a session in his or her turn. However, when I understood the challenges of contemplation, I came to the conclusion that too much equality among group members was not conducive to contemplation. Not everybody is equally experienced and skilled in facilitating – you cannot expect a first-time facilitator to conduct a great a session like an experienced one. Group facilitators are somewhat like music conductors who conduct an orchestra, and their personal abilities are indispensable for a well-orchestrated session. Their role is to guide the participants through a sequence of exercises, set the proper rhythm and pace, and cultivate the contemplative atmosphere. Only when the activity flows seamlessly, can the participants give themselves fully to the contemplative "polyphony."

I therefore decided to take the lead and manage most of the philosophical sessions by myself. I started to assemble a repertoire of contemplative exercises under titles such as "precious speaking" (a technique for expressing your insight in a precise and condensed way), "gentle reading" (breaking the usual flow of reading in order to savor individual words), and so on. I used the name "philosophical companionship" to refer to any group engaged in this activity.

I conducted several online philosophical companionships and invited new fellow philosophical practitioners to participate in them. Each companionship was limited to four sessions, one session per week, in order not to let the activity dwindle over time and lose energy. Gradually the sessions became intense and structured, offering the participants precious experiences, insights, and a sense of group-togetherness.

Philosophical retreats

I continued to direct those online philosophical companionships for several months with participants from several countries. And then, a new idea started intriguing me: organizing a contemplative retreat somewhere in Europe, where many of my colleagues lived. This, however, was not an easy task, given that I was living in the USA.

In 2016, friends of friends generously allowed me to use their summer house in northwest Italy, in the wooded mountains of Liguria. I was enthusiastic. I organized a weekend retreat of philosophical contemplation with the help of Stefania Giordano, a fellow philosophical practitioner from Italy. Sixteen people from four European countries participated in this retreat. The participants' enthusiastic feedback encouraged me to continue.

And then a new door opened: One of the participants, Michele Zese, offered me the use of his family house for future retreats. This house, in the tiny village of Brando on the mountains near Torino, proved to be crucial for future developments. The first retreat in Brando, in September of 2017, was deep and inspiring. At the end of the retreat, seven of us remained for an extra morning. We sat around the kitchen table, satisfied and full of impressions, reflecting together. There and then we decided to form a group devoted to philosophical contemplation, which we later named "Deep Philosophy."

This new international group started meeting online regularly, and it also organized several subsequent retreats in Brando and elsewhere. We experimented with new techniques and created a training program for new members. New members joined us, while others left (as is expected in any active, intensive group). The result was a nucleus of about six or seven full members, as well as a larger circle of people from various countries who occasionally participated in our online and retreat activities.

These events taught me another important lesson: that developing a new format of activities is a long process. It takes time and experimentation for a new approach to consolidate and find its optimal form.

This, in fact, is the main reason why I am telling here about these experiments in such detail. Deep Philosophy is not an arbitrary invention but a result of a long dynamic, creative process which kept growing in the course of several years. Although it was nurtured by the creative efforts of committed members, it had a life of its own which transcended our initial thoughts. The fruits of this process can serve as witnesses to the fact that contemplative philosophy, and Deep Philosophy in particular, are expressions of the human quest for a deep meaningful encounter with life.

Theory of Deep Philosophy

The Deep Philosophy group continued meeting regularly online, as well as in occasional retreats, and within a few months it developed a repertoire of contemplative-philosophical techniques. Soon the need arose to consolidate this practice around basic principles, and to give it a theoretical foundation. As practitioners we wanted to have a better conception of what we were doing.

Several issues presented themselves as especially important: First, what does "inner depth" mean? The expression is associated with a powerful inner experience which one experiences while contemplating, but what can we say about it theoretically?

Second, what exactly are we doing when we contemplate? What happens to us when we think about a text from our inner depth?

Third, what is the relationship among group members during the session, and between the practitioners and the author of the text? In practice we felt that we were "resonating" with each other and with the text, and experiencing a strong sense of togetherness. But what is the nature of this togetherness or resonating?

Fourth, what can we hope to achieve through this practice? To be sure, we experienced a profound sense of meaningfulness and preciousness, and we were confident about the value of what we were doing. But how could we conceptualize the significance of this activity?

These and related issues were on my mind for several months. I often searched in traditional philosophical writings for philosophical ideas that could help develop a theoretical foundation. I found especially helpful texts by the ancient Stoics and Neo-Platonists, German Romanticists, American Transcendentalists, several Existentialists, as well as a number of 20th Century thinkers such as Bergson and Buber. But it was not until 2018 and 2019 that a conceptual picture started taking a clear shape in my mind, and a solid network of ideas emerged.

As a result, we now have a theoretical and methodological framework of Deep Philosophy. True to the historical nature of philosophy, it is inspired by ideas of selected philosophers from the past, but it also goes beyond them to form a new and unique vision. This network of ideas and practices plays an important role in the training that we give to people who wish to join us and become facilitators themselves. Several such training courses have already ended successfully, and as new people join us, they bring with them new energies and perspectives.

It should be clear from the above historical account that the theory, methodology, and practice of Deep Philosophy are the fruit of an intense process of ongoing investigation. We hope that it will keep evolving and never petrify. Deep Philosophy views itself not as a final truth, but as always being in a dynamic process of growth.

Chapter 7

HISTORICAL ROOTS

Deep Philosophy is both new and old. In one sense it started emerging in the early 2000s and was consolidated in 2017-2020 by a small international group of philosophical practitioners who called themselves The Deep Philosophy Group. In another sense, it has older historical roots, some going back to ancient philosophy. Indeed, philosophers throughout the history of philosophy have served as important sources of inspiration for practitioners of Deep Philosophy.

Historical roots: Philosophical methods

The philosophical methods which we use in Deep Philosophy have a special contemplative character. They create a discourse that is very different from the intellectual discussions practiced by most mainstream academic philosophers nowadays and by many philosophers of the past. Nevertheless, methodological themes that are similar to ours can be found throughout the history of philosophy.

One such historical theme, found in Deep Philosophy too, is based on the idea that discursive or intellectual thinking is not sufficient for understanding fundamental aspects of our world. Alternative forms of thinking – holistic, poetic, intuitive, contemplative, etc. – are needed in order to comprehend human experience, human life, or reality in general. Proponents of this view include Neo-Platonists such as Plotinus (204-270 AD) and Proclus (412-485 AD), who practiced meditative techniques to connect to higher levels of reality; German Romanticists such as Novalis (1772-1801) and Friedrich Schlegel (1772-1829), who believed that poetic and intuitive forms of thinking are necessary for a comprehensive understanding of the world; Henri Bergson (1859-1941), who contended that only a special holistic intuition can appreciate the real nature of our experiences; and Edmond Husserl (1859-1938), who developed a special kind of introspection to understand the fundamental structure of experience. Deep Philosophy shares this desire to go beyond intellectual discussions, and in this respect it is similar to those approaches.

A second historical theme, also found in Deep Philosophy, is based on the understanding that deep philosophizing requires the cultivation of a special state of mind. Understanding reality is not just a matter of "look and see," because you may not yet have the mental or spiritual capacities to "see." The desired kind of understanding is possible only after you have developed special sensitivities. Thinkers who espoused this theme include Plato (about 424-348 BC), whose dialogue "The symposium" describes how the philosopher rises, in a long and difficult process, through several levels of erotic wisdom towards the appreciation of the One; the ancient Stoics such as Marcus Aurelius (121-180 AD), who used spiritual exercises of writing, inner dialogue, and imagery in order to connect to their true self (so-called guiding faculty) and develop a deeper awareness of life and the cosmos; Baruch Spinoza (1632-1677), who described what he called "intellectual love of God" (or the "third kind of knowledge") as the highest level of wisdom and understanding one can reach after years of philosophical work; and Ralph Waldo Emerson (1803–1882), who called his readers and listeners to develop inner sensitivities to the metaphysical source of inspiration which he called "The Over-soul."

A third methodological theme, found in Deep Philosophy and in some historical philosophers, is the idea that different historical philosophies need not be treated as mutually contradictory claims to truth, as they might seem to be. This approach sometimes takes the shape of pluralism or syncretism, and suggests that different philosophies can be understood as different expressions of the same human understandings or experiences. For Deep Philosophy, different philosophical voices are not just consistent with each other but complement each other into a rich human polyphony.

These examples demonstrate that Deep Philosophy has methodological principles that resemble those of important historical approaches. Although none of these approaches is, strictly speaking, the same as Deep Philosophy, they can be considered as its cousins, or historical roots.

Historical roots: The power of philosophizing

From another historical perspective, we find similarities between the way various earlier thinkers understood the power of philosophizing and the way it is understood in Deep Philosophy. Those earlier thinkers believed that philosophy is not limited to producing abstract theories, because it can influence us in deeper ways.

One historical example, central to Deep Philosophy, is the idea that philosophy can help us go beyond the boundaries of normal thinking and reveal hidden aspects of reality that are not normally accessible to us. This idea can be found in some of the philosophers already mentioned above, for example Plato and the Neo-Platonists, who believed that there are higher levels of reality, beyond the material world, that require a special kind contemplative thinking to be appreciated. Plato's Allegory of the Cave nicely illustrates the idea that the philosopher must step out of the "cave" of ordinary thinking in order to see beyond mere shadows of reality. An interesting modern example is Karl Jaspers (1883-1969) who argued that philosophical systems (as well as myths, nature, and art) can serve as "ciphers" of Transcendence that point us beyond our objective world and its subject-object structure. Likewise, the theologian and philosopher Paul Tillich (1886-1965) contended that cultural creations, including philosophy, can serve as "symbols" that refer us to realms to which we have no other access, opening them to us and us to them.

Second, for many philosophers throughout the ages, philosophizing has transformative powers. By means of philosophizing we can attain a higher or deeper state of mind, more whole, free, or harmonious. Examples are most of the prominent thinkers mentioned above. From this perspective, the role of philosophy is not just to produce ideas and theories, but to change us.

Sometimes this theme is expressed in terms of self-transformation: While in everyday life we are normally controlled by rigid psychological patterns that make our life superficial, fragmentary, and automatic, philosophy helps us transcend this prison. It can help us transform ourselves, at least in part or temporarily, to become more integrated, free, and connected to the true fountains of our being. An obvious example is Stoic philosophers such as Epictetus (50-135 AD) and Marcus Aurelius (121-180 AD) whose goal was to liberate us from our attachments and attain inner freedom.

In a somewhat different direction, some philosophers held that philosophizing can lead to a long-term development of our basic attitude to life. Most of the above-mentioned philosophers shared this conviction. Additional examples include Epicurus (341-270 BC) who believed that philosophy can guide us to a life of simplicity and quiet happiness; Jean-Jacques Rousseau (1712-1778) whose philosophy instructs us how to cultivate our authentic self; and Friedrich Nietzsche (1844-1900) whose poetic philosophy aims at inspiring us to go through the difficult process of overcoming our small self towards living a fuller and nobler life.

These examples demonstrate that unlike theoretical thinkers from ancient times to contemporary academic philosophers, many other historical philosophers believed that the power of philosophy is much greater than merely composing abstract theories. In this respect, they resemble the aspirations of Deep Philosophy.

Historical precursors of Deep Philosophy

The historical themes mentioned above appear in the writings of diverse thinkers who lived in different historical periods and had different worldviews. Naturally they expressed these themes in different ways and by means of different terminologies and concepts. They may be regarded as precursors to Deep Philosophy, and some have actually inspired the Deep Philosophy Group. The following is an incomplete list of some of those precursors, organized more or less chronologically:

Plato (427—347 BC) can be regarded as one of our earliest precursors. As he tells us in his dialogue "The Symposium" and in the Allegory of the Cave, the source of philosophy is the yearning – or Eros – for what he called the Good, True, and Beautiful. Philosophy is motivated not by cold intellectual interest but by a yearning, and it leads the true philosophical "lover" not to the accumulation of mere objective knowledge, but to the highest appreciation of "beauty" that makes life worth living. Furthermore, the path towards those heights involves an inner transformation – symbolized by the metaphor of stepping out of a cave, or climbing the steps of love – towards attaining a full understanding of reality. Philosophy, then, is a long path of elevating life.

The next important precursors are the ancient Stoics thinkers. A prominent example is the book *Meditations* by the philosopher and Roman Emperor Marcus Aurelius (121-180 AD), who wrote it as a notebook of spiritual exercises. His exercises include imagery techniques, writing and thinking exercises, speaking to oneself, and exhorting oneself to think and live according to Stoic principles. Many of these exercises were meant to awaken his dormant "guiding principle," or "daemon" – the true self that is in harmony with the Logos of the universe, which is similar to what we call "our inner depth." Evidently, philosophy for Marcus Aurelius was a way of life that required ongoing contemplative exercises aimed at inner change. Here we also find the important distinction between our normal psychological patterns and our true inner self, which it is the task of philosophy to awaken and strengthen.

An important thinker who regarded philosophy as involving contemplative practices was the influential Neo-Platonist philosopher Plotinus (204–270 AD). For him, philosophy helps remind our soul of its higher origin, awaken it from its fallen state, and direct it to rise again towards higher levels of reality. We find in his approach, as in the vision of Deep Philosophy, the distinction between everyday thinking and intuitive understanding of higher reality, as well as the yearning to connect with reality through meditative practices.

The visions of Plato and of Plotinus, that philosophy can help develop in us a higher level of understanding and connect us with higher levels of reality, is found in many later philosophers of Neo-Platonism, which was a major school of thought for more than a thousand years. One interesting Neo-Platonist philosopher of the Renaissance, Pico della Mirandola (1463—1494), held that different historical theories, such as Plato's and Aristotle's, do not contradict each other as they seem to do. Rather, so he claimed, they are different perspectives or formulations of the same truths. This philosophical syncretism is reminiscent of our own approach to historical philosophies. From the perspective of Deep Philosophy too, the apparent contradictions between different philosophical theories are superficial, and we avoid the common academic tendency to see them as opponents fighting over the truth. For us they are different expressions of the same deeper realm, specifically different "voices" of the fundamental human reality. Although our pluralism and Pico's syncretism are not the same, we share with him the appreciation of different philosophical theories as arising from the same deep source, and as different aspects of a common human wisdom.

From another perspective, an important theme in Deep Philosophy is the intimate connection between abstract philosophical ideas and concrete everyday moments of life. In our contemplation sessions we often reflect on how our text resonates with participants' personal experiences. A similar motivation can be found in the French philosopher Michel de Montaigne (1533-1592) whose major book *Essays* weaves together anecdotes and personal stories, quotations from ancient thinkers, and his own philosophical insights and ideas. For us, as for him, philosophical ideas need not be separate from everyday life, because the two can be woven most intimately together.

The awareness of higher forms of understanding continues in various forms in modern philosophy. Thus, for example, we find in Benedict Spinoza (1632—1677), an important Jewish Dutch philosopher, the view that philosophy can lead us to a higher state of mind and wisdom – "the third kind of knowledge" as he calls it – which involves inner peace and joy.

The distinction between ordinary and higher dimensions of our being can also be found in the writings of the influential Swiss-French philosopher Jean-Jacques Rousseau (1712—1778). Rousseau distinguishes between one's social self, which is the superficial mask that we normally wear without being aware of it, and the natural self, which is the original spontaneous energies with which we are born. Society pressures us into adopting a false social self, thus making us alienated from our true self. Proper education, however, can cultivate the natural self and shield it from negative influences like a young plant in a greenhouse. Although in Deep Philosophy we do not subscribe to the pessimistic view that society necessarily alienates the individual, we nevertheless find inspiration in Rousseau's project of reconnecting ourselves with an original, deeper dimension of ourselves.

An interesting precursor to our practice of philosophizing in togetherness is found among German Romanticist philosophers, especially Novalis (1772-1801) and Friedrich Schlegel (1772-1829). They often practiced writing in togetherness: Each thinker would write his own fragments, and when the fragments of different writers were put together, the result was a network of ideas that transcended any individual author. They called this practice "Symphilosophy," which is reminiscent of our practice of resonating with each other while philosophizing in togetherness. These Romanticists are also relevant to Deep Philosophy in another respect, namely the profound connection which they saw between philosophical thinking and poetic thinking. In line with their approach, many of our contemplative practices are based on the realization that when we formulate our philosophical ideas in a poetic fashion, the result is a different form of thinking that is deep and inspired.

Another poetic philosopher from a slightly later period is Ralph Waldo Emerson (1803—1882), leader of the American Transcendentalist movement. Especially relevant to us is his idea of the Over-Soul – a source of creative insights and inspiration that transcends our normal individual self. In Deep Philosophy we share with Emerson the task of opening ourselves inwardly to this source of wisdom, or what we call "inner depth," which is beyond our normal psychological structures and that inspires us with insights.

Existentialist philosophies have several themes in common with Deep Philosophy, especially the connection they see between philosophy and the individual's concrete life. For Søren Kierkegaard (1813—1855), father of Existentialism, philosophical life-issues cannot be separated from the individual's "subjective" life. Objective theories and truths are of little interest to him, because truth is a matter of personal passion, commitment, and choice, and these require self-awareness, authenticity, and seriousness. In Deep Philosophy we share Kierkegaard's view that authentic philosophy must emerge from one's personal relationship with life, rather than from abstract thinking.

Karl Jaspers (1883—1969), a German existentialist philosopher and psychiatrist, explains that our thinking objectifies the world, and it is therefore blind to the fundamental reality that is more primordial than objects and objectification, a realm which he calls "the encompassing" (also translated as "the comprehensive") because it encompasses both subject and object. For him, great philosophical texts can act as "ciphers" that point us towards this original reality, although we can never capture it in our thoughts.

A similar view is expressed by the German-American thinker Paul Tillich (1886—1965) who holds that ideas can function as "symbols" that take us beyond themselves towards dimensions of reality that cannot be accessed directly. In Deep Philosophy we share with Jaspers and Tillich the understanding that philosophical ideas can serve not just as theories about the objective world, but also as pointers that direct us beyond objective descriptions to a fundamental reality.

In a somewhat similar fashion, the French existentialist philosopher Gabriel Marcel (1889-1963) holds that a central dimension of human life is a "mystery," in the sense that it cannot be grasped from the perspective of an objective observer. We can appreciate these dimensions only by taking part in them and living them authentically, but not by theorizing about them. Like Marcel, in Deep Philosophy we seek to relate to the personal dimension of our being which cannot be accessed through intellectual thinking alone.

Outside existentialism, the French philosopher Henri Bergson (1859—1941) argues that if we carefully examine our inner mental life, we will realize that it is a holistic flow that cannot be analyzed into separate elements and captured in descriptions. Like a symphony that is more than the sum of individual sounds, the deeper layers of our consciousness are a stream of always-novel holistic qualities that interpenetrate each other and cannot be broken down into parts. Yet, we are able to appreciate our deep experiences with another faculty: our intuition. In Deep Philosophy, too, we seek to appreciate the deep aspects of our inner life in a non-analytic and non-descriptive way, although our main method is contemplation.

For Martin Buber (1878—1965), a Jewish Austrian-Israeli philosopher, human reality is constituted by our relationships to others, not by our separate individual selves. Fundamentally we are always persons-in-relation, so that in our authentic way of being we are in togetherness with others, with nature, with God, and even with the voices of dead thinkers. In Deep Philosophy, too, we find significance in the power of togetherness, and we implement it in our practice of resonating in togetherness with our companions and with historical thinkers.

The philosophy of Maria Zambrano (1904-1991), a poetic Spanish thinker, focuses on those aspects of our mental life that emerge from regions beyond reason – from dreams, reveries, delirium, poetic thinking. To appreciate those non-rational facets of our world we need to cultivate a special inner space, or "clearing in the forest," through which we may receive unexpected insights about the hidden deep layers of our reality. Like her, in Deep Philosophy we recognize the limitation of rational analysis and the need to go beyond it.

Additional philosophers can be added to the list, but the bottom line is clear: Deep Philosophy is not an altogether new invention, nor is it foreign to the spirit of traditional philosophy. It has deep roots throughout the history of Western thought.

Part C

PILLARS OF DEEP PHILOSOPHY

The practice of Deep Philosophy is embedded in a body of theoretical ideas which are not easy to summarize in one unitary theory. Like many human activities, Deep Philosophy grew out of a variety of different insights, personal experiences, and visions, and the result is a network of ideas that are woven together in complex ways. Nevertheless, several central principles can be identified in it and formulated clearly. These are what we call "The Pillars of Deep Philosophy."

Chapter 8

SUMMARY OF THE SEVEN PILLARS OF DEEP PHILOSOPHY

The seven pillars of Deep Philosophy revolve around seven concepts: Yearning for realness, Inner depth, Philosophy, Contemplation, Resonating in Togetherness, Voices of Reality, and Transformation.

Pillar 1: Yearning for realness

We encounter the first pillar when we experience a yearning for truth, for ultimate reality, for the foundation of existence, or (since these words have been over-used) for what we call "realness." When we yearn for realness we do not seek pleasurable experiences or happiness for ourselves, nor do we want to satisfy our intellectual curiosity. A yearning is more like love than like a desire for satisfaction: Like a lover who adores the beloved – not his own pleasant experiences! – so that his heart "goes out" to the beloved, likewise when we yearn for realness we seek to move beyond our self-interest towards what is precious, real, fundamental. Yearning, like love, is an act of devotion, a going beyond oneself.

Deep Philosophy is born out of this yearning. Without this yearning, with only a desire for satisfactory experiences, there can be no Deep Philosophy.

Pillar 2: Inner depth

We sense realness in certain special states of mind which are fundamentally different from our ordinary everyday moments (although the distinction is not sharp, and may be a matter of degree and mixture). These states have a special quality of inner unity, intense presence, and fullness. When we experience them we sense that our entire being is present, and not just an isolated thought or feeling, and that they take place in an inner dimension within us that is beyond our familiar self. They are often accompanied by a sense of preciousness, plenitude, and realness. In comparison, ordinary moments are fragmented, half-conscious, dull.

Hence, these experiences are special not just in *what* we experience but in *how* we experience, or to put it differently, in "where" within us the experience takes place, or which dimension of our being is doing the experiencing. In Deep Philosophy we call this inner dimension, which is awakened only in such special moments, "inner depth."

The distinction between deep and superficial states of mind, even if not sharp, has important implications for Deep Philosophy, because it means that in our quest for realness we must transform our normal states of mind. Our usual mental states are not enough, and to practice Deep Philosophy we must change them with the help of special contemplative exercises.

Pillar 3: Philosophy

It is possible that there are several different ways to attain the sense of realness we are seeking, among them perhaps special kinds of poetry, music, and religious rituals. But our own way is philosophical, because our goal is not just to experience but to understand, not just to enjoy images and feelings but to comprehend fundamental aspects of life and the world. This is why we work with philosophical ideas – because they deal with fundamental reality. Without the attempt to understand reality philosophically, a practice is not Deep Philosophy, as valuable as it might be.

In order to cultivate our philosophical understandings, we must speak and think in the language of fundamental reality. Such a language cannot be limited to specific objects, people, facts or events, as in newspapers, history books, or scientific articles. The language of fundamental reality consists of fundamental ideas before they have been restricted to specific objects, and this is the language to which philosophy traditionally aspires.

Combining all this with the previous pillar, we may say that Deep Philosophy is a philosophical exploration of fundamental ideas, which employs thinking from our inner depth.

Pillar 4: Contemplation

Discursive thinking – the normal, everyday way in which we think – is not suitable for our philosophical search for realness. What characterizes this kind of thinking is the structure of thinking-about: I think "about" some object of thought – whether real or imaginary, material or abstract, present or past or expected. Metaphorically, I place before my mind an object of thought, and I inspect it from the outside. Thus I separate myself from the reality in question, I turn it into an object for me, and I become an external observer, remote and uninvolved. This cannot put me in intimate touch with the realness of that reality, which is the goal of Deep Philosophy.

In order to avoid the discursive mode of thinking (or "thinking-about"), in Deep Philosophy we adopt a different mode of thinking called contemplation. In contemplation we seek to make reality present within us, instead of trying to think "about" it. We "embody" it within ourselves, just as, by analogy, we may embody within ourselves a sense of love or happiness instead of thinking about them.

To do so, we must think from a dimension of our being that lies beyond our ordinary psychological "aboutness" mechanisms, namely our inner depth. Contemplation is, therefore, thinking from our inner depth, thus making the reality in question present within us.

Contemplation is not easy to practice, since it goes against our automatic tendency to think-about. That is why we use special contemplative techniques – to push aside our normal thinking patterns and give rise to contemplative thinking instead.

Pillar 5: Resonating in Togetherness

Traditionally, philosophers' main task has been to compose theories about reality. As a result, communication between philosophers has been largely a debate about which ideas (or theories) are acceptable or unacceptable, true or false.

This kind of discourse is not suitable for Deep Philosophy, since it expresses a form of intellectual thinking-about. In Deep Philosophy we use a different form of communication: Resonating. In resonating, we do not make any claim about which ideas are true or false, and we do not judge or evaluate each other's words. Rather, we listen to the meanings that others express and "resonate" with them by responding to them with our own meanings.

Resonating is analogous to the way jazz musicians improvise music together. The saxophone does not play *about* what the piano has played, and the trumpet does not agree or disagree with the bass. Instead, they acknowledge each other by resonating with each other's musical phrases, complementing them and responding to them, creating a rich music together.

Resonating can be done from the state of mind of inner depth, but not necessarily so. We can also resonate with each other in a joking or playful mood for example. But when we resonate from our inner depth, a new kind of relationship is formed between us: We now speak from beyond our usual self, from a common polyphony of meanings that encompasses us all. This relationship is called *togetherness*.

Being in your inner depth is a state of mind, resonating is a form of communication, and togetherness is a kind of relationship. Although these three are not the same, they are intimately connected.

Pillar 6: Voices of Reality

When we contemplate on a philosophical text, our purpose is not just to understand what it says. If this was our purpose, an intellectual discussion would have been enough. We contemplate on philosophical ideas because by means of them we go beyond them, to discern deep meanings that appear in our inner depth. In this sense, philosophical ideas serve as doors to the depth.

"Ideas" are not the same as "meanings." Ideas, in the normal sense of the term, are elements of discursive discourse – contents of our mind which we use to explain, theorize, discuss, and which we transmit to each other. As such, they are part of the structure of thinking-about. In contrast, deep meanings are not things in our mind and are not "about" anything. They are reality itself – or more precisely, aspects or qualities of reality – before it has been structured as objects of our thinking. They are more primordial than the subject-object structure of the mind.

In order to relate to these fundamental meanings we let them manifest themselves within us. And when we do so, we are no longer thinking about reality and its meanings from the outside, but are witnessing them intimately with us. We call these fundamental meanings "voices of reality"; or, to acknowledge our limited human perspective, "voices of human reality."

The contemplator's sense of realness, of presence, preciousness, and plenitude attest to our intimate connection with those voices of reality.

Pillar 7: Transformation

Our sense of realness and preciousness during contemplation, and our sense of thinking and speaking from our inner depth, indicate that something significant is being transformed within us. In moments of deep contemplation I am no longer a thinker inspecting objects of thought from the outside; I am immersed in an inner space where I am encompassed by fundamental meanings.

Of course, I do not lose myself completely in that alternate space; I do not forget that I am sitting on a chair with a book in my hands. Yet, on a certain level of my awareness, in a certain dimension of my being, I enter a realm of fundamental meanings. I am now a wave in the ocean, embodying its movements within me.

In this sense, during contemplation a certain aspect of our being is being transformed. However, this powerful experience does not normally last for long. Once we stop contemplating, we are back to our normal state of mind. Yet, our inner depth does not completely disappear. Even though we may no longer experience it strongly, it may still continue in the back of our mind.

Practicing contemplation on a regular basis helps us keep awake our inner depth even beyond the session, at least to some extent. The more we think and feel and act from our inner depth, the less we do so from our automatic psychological patterns. Although the practice of contemplation will likely not completely replace our personality with a new enlightened one, it can nevertheless cultivate an additional dimension to our inner life.

Chapter 9

REFLECTIONS ON THE PILLARS OF DEEP PHILOSOPHY

1. Beyond remoteness
(Reflection on Pillar 1: Yearning for Realness)

Our everyday world is remote. I perceive people and objects around me at a physical distance from me. I always perceive them "out there," situated outside my body and sense organs. I can think about them, I can see their shape or hear their sound or feel their texture, but I am always separated from them. I am remote even from myself – whenever I think about myself, my thoughts about myself turn me into an object of thought.

Thus we live in the mode of remoteness. As a result, we feel the dullness of everyday life, its alienated indifference, its remote objectivity. "Facts," "objects," "things" – these words refer to this remoteness.

Normally we take this remoteness for granted. What else could we possibly expect? Yet, we long to overcome this remoteness and achieve a greater sense of realness. In response we sometimes look for titillating experiences, for excitement or for passion, we try to merge with ideologies and social movements, but these are not real answers to the lack of realness. They offer us the "high" of feelings or experiences, but not real realness. What we crave is a radically different way of being in the world, one that is not at a distance.

Indeed, in special moments – in nature, in togetherness with another person, in contemplation, in spiritual experiences – we sometimes sense a powerful presence of marvelous realness, or at least a taste of it. We may describe it afterwards in a peculiar way: "I was deeply touched," "I felt it deep inside me," "I was invaded by a sense of presence," "I was completely opened to the world." Such expressions suggest that our sense of separateness dissolved for a few moments. What we witnessed was not a remote "something" outside us, not an object of thought or perception over there, but the realness of reality in our own intimate being. It was as if the distinction between inside and outside started melting away.

This sense of realness is not, of course, a new discovery. In the writings of mystics and poets throughout history, as well as spiritual thinkers of virtually all religious traditions, we find reports of such experiences of wondrous realness, as well as the yearning for them. In Deep Philosophy we share this yearning, although not in the name of religious faith or poetic beauty, but because we want to overcome our separation and dull unrealness, and take part in reality as fully as humanly possible.

2. Understanding by embodying
(Reflection on Pillar 2: Inner Depth)

The sense of intense realness which we experience in moments of philosophical contemplation is not a mere feeling. It also involves an understanding that comes to us from the philosophical text we are contemplating.

This is not an ordinary kind of understanding. It is not the usual "understanding-about" of a thought about some topic, but a surge of meanings that engulf me and fill me in their realness. Like a wave in an ocean I come to embody within myself the movements of the ocean of meanings. A wave does not "look at" or "think about" the ocean from a distance; it discerns its motion within itself. This is an understanding by embodying, not by representing.

That is the kind of understanding we seek in contemplation. By pushing aside our psychological self, we open an inner space where meanings can manifest themselves in all their realness. We then witness the text's meanings in a dimension of ourselves that transcends our normal thinking structures.

We call this dimension our "inner depth." The metaphor of "depth" comes from the image of a hidden subterranean fountain or root. Like a fountain of water that emerges from the depth of the earth, and like the underground root of a tree that gives birth to the visible tree, our inner depth is the hidden dimension of our being that is at the foundation of our understanding. It is more primordial than our thinking-about psychological mechanisms, before our reality is split into subject and object.

3a. Philosophical ideas as doors to the foundation
(Reflection on Pillar 3: Philosophy)

In the broadest sense of "text contemplation," one may contemplate on any kind text, even on a history book, a romantic novel, or a newspaper column. If contemplation simply means reading a text silently and listening to it inwardly, then the text need not be deep or philosophical. Nevertheless, there is something special about philosophical texts that takes contemplation to an altogether different level. And here contemplation means something much more specific.

Philosophy works with general ideas – the general idea of friendship (not just Mary's particular friendship), the idea of freedom (not Joe's free act yesterday), and so on. In contrast, a history book or newspaper article deals with particular things and events: a certain person or family, a particular nation, a geographical location, a historical war or street protest. Furthermore, philosophical ideas are fundamental ideas, in the sense that they relate to the foundation of our world.

In a certain sense, general or fundamental ideas can be found not just in philosophical texts but even in popular slogans or love songs ("Love is all you need," for instance, meaning that love is a basic human need). But there is a big difference here. Philosophy always works with more than a single isolated statement. It seeks to compose a rich network of ideas that expresses a complex perspective on life or reality, in other words a worldview. Indeed, once you enrich a popular slogan into a complex network of ideas, the result may be a philosophy.

In short, philosophy works with networks of general ideas of fundamental aspects of reality. Contemplating on a philosophical text, therefore, amounts to "stepping into" a worldview shaped by general, fundamental ideas. We may even say "Stepping into a world," because when I truly contemplate on a text, I do not *think about* it as I do when I analyze it intellectually, but rather let the fundamental meanings of the text envelop me like a world. I enter it somewhat as I enter the world of a novel, or of a movie, or a game.

In this sense, philosophical theories serve as doors through which contemplators can enter the realm of the foundation of human reality – provided they do not think about it intellectually, but contemplate on it from the inside.

3b. Philosophizing beyond theories
(Reflection on Pillar 3: Philosophy)

Deep Philosophy is rooted in the historical tradition of Western philosophy, and it shares its central characteristics. First, like virtually all philosophers of the past, we as practitioners of Deep Philosophy address fundamental issues of life and reality. Second, like all historical philosophers, we work on networks of ideas in order to shed light on these fundamental issues. Third, like them we employ primarily the powers of the mind, as opposed to blind faith on the one hand, and empirical (scientific) observations on the other hand. Naturally, historical philosophers used a wider variety of powers of the mind – logical analysis, common sense, intuition, introspection, etc., while we use only some of them, namely contemplative thinking. Lastly, like them we develop our ideas in dialogue with previous philosophers.

These four characteristics apply to virtually every philosopher in the history of Western philosophy. Those thinkers who diverged from them are not regarded as philosophers and are not part of the philosophical tradition. Since Deep Philosophy shares these characteristics, it is, in this sense, part of that historical tradition.

In other respects, however, our practice as Deep Philosophers is different from mainstream philosophy: Whereas virtually all philosophers of the past worked to construct theories that convey truths about reality, for us theories are not important as expressing truths. We have great interest in philosophical writings, but not in their aspiration to accurately represent reality. We cherish texts that are deep, but not necessarily their claim for truth; texts that bring us in contact with the foundation, not ones that provide us with abstract descriptions of it. Theories (or networks of ideas) are for us an intermediate step on the way to the real goal, namely taking part in the ocean of reality.

3c. Meanings versus ideas
(Reflection on Pillar 3: Philosophy)

If we search for realness, why do we contemplate on philosophical ideas? Philosophical ideas seem abstract and remote, so how can they bring us closer to living reality?

Here we should distinguish between philosophical *ideas* and *meanings*. Ideas are indeed remote because they are "things in our mind" – conceptual items which we manipulate in our thinking, record in writing and transfer from one person to another. One might distinguish between different kinds of ideas – concepts (such as the concept of "horse" of "justice"), statements (such as "The sun is shining"), explanations, theories, etc. – but they all have something important in common: They are abstract items in our mind that signify (represent, refer to) the world outside them.

The distance between ideas and what they signify means that their ability to connect us with reality is severely limited. As long as we think with ideas, our thoughts are "about" reality and relate to it from a distance. For this reason, philosophical ideas do not interest us in themselves. They interest us only to the extent that we can transcend them.

This is what we do in Deep Philosophy. We use philosophical ideas in order to go beyond ideas. Through those ideas we go to the foundation that gives birth to them, namely human reality. But by "human reality" we don't mean material objects such as stones and trees and molecules, but rather fundamental meanings (or qualities) before our mind objectifies them into objects of thought.

We experience the difference between ideas and meanings in contemplation sessions: We often have a strong sense of meaningfulness, but we are unable to translate it into definite ideas. We sense it as more primordial than our concepts, as transcending our linguistic and conceptual units.

Philosophical contemplation embodies in our minds this barely describable fundamental reality (in the sense of the fundamental meanings that compose it). This should not be too surprising. Reality, after all, is already in us – we are part of it like a wave in the ocean, and it can surge in us just as the movements of the ocean surge in a wave. Contemplation can evoke in us not just a representation of the original movement but the original movement itself.

To use a different metaphor, philosophical contemplation can make reality "speak" in us in its original voices. Unlike ideas, fundamental meanings are not abstractions, but rather reality itself "speaking" in us. They become abstractions only once we turn them into ideas about something, into a concept or a theory for example. But meanings in themselves – meanings before we start thinking about them and objectifying them – are the "sounds" that compose the "music" of our lives.

That is why we work with philosophical ideas, and why we use texts that are philosophical. Philosophy is a discourse of fundamental ideas, and such ideas can manifest in us fundamental meanings – if we only learn to attend to them.

4a. Contemplation as self-transcending
(Reflection on Pillar 4: Contemplation)

We contemplate because we strive to overcome the limitations of our ordinary patterns of thinking which have the structure of thinking-about: Our thought selects a specific object-of-thought (a person, an event, an idea, or whatever the thought is about), in isolation from the rest of the world, and asserts something about it – for example, "This tree is tall," or "Love is an intense emotion."

This form of thinking is useful when we deal with specific objects in our world, but it is inappropriate when we want to relate to the deeper realm of primordial meanings. Since it views reality through the lens of objectified items, it cannot deal with reality before it has been objectified, before it has been shaped by our psychological structures and turned into objects of thought.

The role of contemplation is to allow us to transcend these structures. Experience tells us that when we contemplate, we no longer think with our usual objectifying psychology, and that what is doing the thinking is another dimension of our being. There is no need to speculate about what this dimension is, but we can note that it exists: We are indeed able to think from a pre-objective, primordial dimension of ourselves, or what we call our inner depth.

The problem is that this is not easy to do. We cannot activate our depth at will, since it is not governed by the self's psychological mechanisms. In order to contemplate we must push aside our psychological self, force it to give up control, and wait for our inner depth to speak.

But even this is not easy to do. We cannot avoid our normal thinking patterns – our "automatic pilot" – just by wanting to avoid it. We need techniques to help us. As contemplators we use a variety of contemplative methods to suppress our ordinary psychological thinking patterns and open instead a "clearing" – an inner space of silent attentiveness – that is relatively free from our normal psychological activity.

The result is a very different form of thinking that emerges from a more primordial source within us, and that yields much deeper meanings than our psychology-based concepts and ideas. Although these meanings are not as sharp and well-defined as objects of thought, they are not limited to discursive patterns of thinking. That is why in contemplation we often experience ourselves sensing meanings we cannot describe, being flooded by insights of intensity and realness which objects of thought cannot give us, or expanding beyond our familiar boundaries.

4b. The power of contemplation
(Reflection on Pillar 4: Contemplation)

Text-contemplation has a special power to make deep meanings intensely present to us. This power is due not just to *what* we contemplate but primarily to *how* we do so, in other words not just to the philosophical content itself but mainly to the state of mind with which we relate to it. Intellectual thinking has a limited power to change us because it gives us only objects of thought while leaving us unchanged. Contemplation, in contrast, impacts us because it changes the thinking act too, and the mind itself.

When I contemplate on a philosophical text, what is present to me is not objects of thought such as ideas or concepts, but pre-objectified meanings that are neither in the object nor in the subject. They fill my inner space entirely, appearing neither as subjective nor as objective, and brimming with realness. These meanings, indeed, are aspects of reality – not thoughts about reality nor representations of reality, but reality itself incarnated in me, real meanings in their realness.

As a helpful metaphor, I may imagine myself as a wave in the ocean of fundamental meanings. The movements of the water of the ocean are in the wave which is me. Just as there is no distance between the wave and the water of the ocean, there is no distance between me and the meanings of reality. I am in those fundamental meanings and they are in me. Indeed, I *am* the water of fundamental meanings and the water is me.

From the perspective of this metaphor, when we contemplate on philosophical ideas we step into an ocean of meanings. We step, in other words, into an alternate reality, different from our ordinary world of material things.

Here we use a remarkable human capacity: to enter alternate realities. When we watch a movie or read a novel, we enter an imaginary world and experience it from within as if we were inside it. As we follow the characters and the plot, we feel scared or relieved, hopeful or disappointed, as if the events were happening to us or around us. Importantly, however, we do not get completely lost in this alternate world. We do not confuse the characters on the screen with the person sitting next to us. An unexpected disturbance can easily tear us out of this alternate reality. Evidently, in the back of our mind we know that it is only a movie or a novel.

In philosophical contemplation, too, we enter an alternate world, but with an important difference: This is not a world of objects such as people and stones and flowers, but of something completely different – pre-objective fundamental meanings. Now we are in an altogether different world-order, which re-shapes the basic dimensions of our own existence.

But not every philosophical text manages to do this. If your text portrays a world made of things, then it will leave you in a world of things, and it will leave you an observer of those things. Not much can then happen if you contemplate on that text. But if the text is deep, if it points to a realm of fundamental meanings that cannot be objectified, then it will reshape you and your relation to the world. Once you step into it with the help of contemplation, you will not be the same person, at least for the duration of the session. You will now be a wave in the ocean, and the realness of the ocean will be embodied in you. You will be in it just as it will be in you, enveloped by a sense of realness and fullness.

Of course, as in the case of watching a movie or reading a book, you will not be completely lost in that alternate reality. In the back of your mind you will be aware of the ordinary world of objects around you, and of yourself as a person reading a text. But part of you will be contemplating, and on that level you will be transformed.

5a. The auditory metaphor
(Reflection on Pillar 5: Resonating)

Mainstream philosophers investigate fundamental aspects of reality by attempting to construct theories about them. The use of theories-about is based on the visual metaphor of "looking at" and "seeing." We imagine reality as a kind of landscape spread out over there in front of us, and a theory as a map or picture that represents this landscape. The purpose of the theory is to correspond to that reality just as a map of a city represents the city streets, or just as a photograph of a face corresponds to the face. When we follow this visual metaphor and seek to represent reality in our thoughts or words, we are in effect relating to it from the perspective of an external viewer.

But the visual metaphor is not our only way of relating to reality. An alternative metaphor is that of "hearing" or "listening." Hearing does not involve a picture-object relationship, because the sound I hear does not resemble the object making the sound, and the details of the former do not correspond to the details of the latter. If I hear a whistle, for instance, I may not even know whether it is coming from a bird or a person or a machine.

Furthermore, listening is not completely an external relation. In hearing I experience a sound coming from the outside into me and resonating in my mind. Indeed, if I want to listen to it carefully, I may close my eyes and attend *inwardly*. The external object producing the sound is hidden from my hearing.

"Listening" is therefore a better metaphor for how we relate to ideas and meanings in philosophical contemplation, although like all metaphors it has its limitations. Just as we listen to a sound, in contemplation we "listen" to ideas as if they are coming into us from somewhere and are now present within us. We then sense them filling our mind, giving us the inner presence which contemplators often experience. "Listening to" ideas is a very different inner attitude from that of "looking at" ideas.

If we follow the auditory metaphor, then ideas in contemplation are analogous to sounds. But the "sounds" we listen to in philosophical contemplation are not empty noises – they also have meanings, as well as an inner structure. We may therefore call them *voices*. Contemplating on a philosophical text is analogous to listening to "voices."

The voices metaphor allows us to distinguish between two elements: first, the sounds; second, the meanings expressed through those sounds. By listening to the text's ideas ("sounds") we are in effect listening to the meanings which those sounds carry. And just as when listening to speech we listen "through" the sounds to the meanings expressed, likewise in contemplation we listen "through" the theoretical ideas to the fundamental meanings that are clothed in them.

Another advantage of the voices metaphor is that it allows us to express the contemplative experience of ideas resounding or "speaking" *within* us. An analogous statement in the visual language of seeing ("seeing within us") makes no sense. Indeed, the auditory metaphor implies that the distinction between inside me and outside me is blurry: Like sounds that we experience both as occurring outside us yet resonating inside us, ideas in contemplation are experienced as being in the text but also resounding in our minds.

Lastly, the auditory metaphor allows us to say that we interact with companions or with texts by "resonating" with them, which is a relationship between voices. The notion of resonating transcends the dichotomies of thinking-about, those of agreeing versus disagreeing, true versus false. These dichotomies govern the visual world of representations-of, of thinking-about, of subject-object. In contrast, the auditory notion of resonating allows contemplators to respond to any given voice with a range of different responses, beyond a simple true-false dichotomy.

5b. Two meanings of resonating
(Reflection on Pillar 5: Resonating)

In contemplation we converse with our text and with each other in a special way – by resonating. The notion of resonating has two meanings. In a broad sense, resonating is a procedure. In a more specific sense, it is a mental state.

As a procedure, resonating means that we respond to the ideas of a person or a text by speaking "alongside" them rather than "about" them. Instead of analyzing them, instead of evaluating or criticizing them, agreeing or disagreeing, we speak with each other like two voices in a concert. Like jazz musicians improvising together, we respond to a companion's phrase with a phrase of our own, we complete each other's melodies or enrich them with harmonies, develop musical themes, and together create a rich symphony of meanings.

But resonating can also mean something internal. As a mental state, it means that I internalize the procedure of resonating and follow it in my mind: I receive ideas into myself without judgment, and I let them hover within me without analyzing or evaluating them. In this state, ideas are no longer statements or theories about the way things are, but meanings that float within me and interact with each other in complex ways.

These interactions create new meaningful qualities, which we experience as precious understandings. Just as the soprano and the tenor create new qualities when they sing together, in an analogous way two meaningful ideas may create new meanings which do not exist in each of them separately.

Resonating makes little sense if we think about ideas as statements-about. In a discourse of true-and-false, you cannot accept at the same time two contradictory statements – for example, that the self is a thinking thing (Descartes) and also that the self is merely a fiction (David Hume). Only one of these two may be accepted as true. But if ideas are voice-like expressions of fundamental meanings, we can accept them both as two voices in a polyphonic choir of meanings, and we can embrace them both.

This does not mean that any idea is just as acceptable as any other idea. Resonating in a "concert" of philosophical meanings is no more arbitrary than resonating in a musical concert: Not every combination creates an equally meaningful result. Its meaningfulness may depend in part on how those particular "voices" interact with each other, and to some extent on contemplators' personal or cultural ways of attending to them.

5c. Deep togetherness
(Reflection on Pillar 5: Resonating)

In group contemplation we resonate in togetherness. Togetherness is related to resonating, but the two are not the same. Resonating is an activity – it is something we do at certain moments by speaking and thinking in certain ways, whereas togetherness is a relationship. We can be in togetherness even when we sit quietly and say nothing, or after the session has ended and we are no longer in contemplation but are still under its influence. Resonating starts at a certain moment and ends at a certain moment – for example, when I interrupt my contemplation to turn on the light or change seats. But our togetherness does not pause for ten seconds just because we are taking a break. Yet, the activity of resonating is very relevant to the relationship of togetherness: It helps create it.

Togetherness in Deep Philosophy should be distinguished from common kinds of being together. In everyday life we often feel together when we enjoy each other's company, as in a picnic with friends. Or, a sports team may act in coordination together to achieve a common goal. Or, a planning team may think and plan together by completing and developing each other's ideas, so that the final result is the product of everybody's contribution.

These kinds of being together – being together in feeling, in acting, in thinking – are common in everyday life, and although they may appear in a Deep Philosophy group, they are not special to it. But there is a deeper kind of togetherness that transcends everyday activity and that can be called "deep togetherness."

In deep togetherness we relate to each other from our inner depth and thus go beyond individual thinking. Together we participate in a realm that transcends our separateness and encompasses us together. This is the shared realm of fundamental meanings, or voices, that inspire us as a group; or, to use a different metaphor, it is the ocean in which we are waves. That is not to deny our individuality or individual differences, but to acknowledge a broader realm that encompasses us all and moves us together.

At the height of contemplation, the boundaries between us dissolve to some extent. More precisely, what dissolves here is not I myself – I do not disappear from the session – but rather the "my-ness" of my thoughts and experiences. The clear boundary that normally separates my thinking from your thinking starts melting away, and my experiences are no longer sharply distinct from yours. I am now a wave in an ocean of meanings side by side with other waves (or companions), no longer the owner of "my" thoughts and experiences, and no longer a separate mind that contains private ideas and feelings. My "I" loses its special status as the center of my world. There is no longer "my" inner depth versus "your" inner depth, but only inner depth.

One might regard this as a kind of self-transcending ecstasy, but this is true only to a limited degree. In fact, this self-transcendence is never complete. As in the case of movie-goers or novel-readers who enter an alternate reality only in one part of their minds, likewise this contemplative ecstasy usually involves only part of our being. While part of me hovers in the realm of fundamental meanings that is beyond my-ness, in the back of my mind I am still an individual self, thinking his own thoughts and communicating with colleagues. Deep togetherness is always partial.

Within this partial deep togetherness, we often notice that ideas appear in our minds as if by themselves, resonating with the text and with each other as if they have a life of their own, speaking by themselves "through" our minds and mouths. The result is a "dis-owned" flow of voices – a symphony without composer, a polyphony of meanings that embraces us all, a reality that is more than the sum of the participants' separate minds.

Deep togetherness, then, is very different from everyday being-together. However, this does not necessarily mean that it produces stronger emotions. Emotions, as valuable as they might be, are part of the world of psychological subjects which we transcend in contemplation, and in themselves they may appear even in situations that have little depth (playing football together for instance, or suffering in prison together). That which is special about deep togetherness takes place on a different level of our being, on the level of voices or fundamental meanings. If we experience anything special in this state, it is not emotions but rather a sense of preciousness and even sacredness, and the realness of the great ocean to which we all belong. These experiences, however intense they may be – whether gentle or powerful, overwhelming or barely perceptible – are the movements of the depth.

6a. Meanings beyond description
(Reflection on Pillar 6: Voices of Reality)

Contemplation allows us to transcend the limits of our ordinary thought. It enables us to relate to those primordial aspects of reality – what we call "voices of human reality" or "fundamental meanings" – that are beyond the reach of our objectifying thinking. If objectifying thought tries to capture those aspects with description, it will inevitably impose on them the structure of subject-about-object, and thus distort them. Contemplation, however, enables us to appreciate them in a non-objectifying way, revealing to us a realm that is not shaped by the subject-object lens.

Thus, the world of objects is not our inescapable prison. That is not to suggest that we have access to ultimate reality. As human beings we are probably restricted by the limitations of our human mind. The point is, rather, that the horizon of human understanding is broader than the horizon of objectifying thought. Our capacity to understand reality is probably limited, but it is richer than our capacity to think-about and talk-about.

The idea that we can appreciate what we cannot capture in description is not in itself surprising. It is reminiscent of how we can appreciate tastes or colors without being able to describe them. How, for example, can you describe the taste of coffee, except very vaguely? To be sure, the analogy with tastes or colors is probably misleading – for one thing, colors are located in objective space whereas meanings are not; but it shows that an inability to describe does not amount to an inability to experience and appreciate.

Still, one might legitimately demand an explanation, as general and vague as it might be, of what those voices or fundamental meanings are.

One immediate answer is: Try contemplating and experience it for yourself. But more can be said here. First, as our contemplative experiences tell us, fundamental meanings are not neutral categories like abstract concepts, but rather qualities of value: We discern their preciousness, at times even sacredness. Preciousness or valuableness is part of what they are. To experience them is to experience them as precious.

Second, as our contemplative experiences tell us, those qualities are generative or creative. They give birth to images, ideas, associations. They are not inert qualities, but a dynamic plenitude.

We may therefore say that fundamental meanings act as fountains of meaning, preciousness, and plenitude. They are a source of what is richly valuable within us, at least for the duration of contemplation.

6b. Voices beyond theory
(Reflection on Pillar 6: Voices of Reality)

When considering the fundamental meanings which we call "voices of reality," we might be tempted to construct a theory about them. We might theorize, for example, that they are like Platonic ideas that determine the essences of all things, and that they are organized in a fixed hierarchy, from the most general idea on top to the more specific ideas in descending order.

This nicely structured theory, however, amounts to turning voices into what they are not – things viewed from the outside. Because describing something, or theorizing about it, means placing it in front of the mind's eye and inspecting it from the perspective of an external observer.

Our contemplative experience reveals something very different: A voice is not a thing to inspect and think about, because it cannot be separated from my thinking act without distortion – it is in the thinking act itself. Once I make it an object of my thought, I have lost it. I am left with a mere semblance of what it had originally been, like a creature of darkness brought to the sunlight in order to observe it.

To appreciate a voice we must bring it into our awareness without "looking" at it, so to speak. We must open a free inner space within us and let it manifest itself there, if it will. This is what we do in contemplation, when we use special exercises to "put" the words of a text in our inner depth and let them "speak" there. We then sense unobjectified meanings appear within us, so that we can think and speak *from* or *with* them, and yet not *about* them.

Here as philosophers we must abandon the pretension that we can squeeze everything into our theories. Any such theory inevitably leaves out those meanings that cannot be objectified, because they involve the subject himself and never go fully to the side of the object.

6c. Voices and inner depth
(Reflection on Pillar 6: Voices of Reality)

In Deep Philosophy we sometimes say that we connect to reality through our "inner depth," while at other times we say that we listen to "voices" of reality. These two expressions, inner depth and voices, come from different languages and use different metaphors, but they are two sides of the same coin. "Depth" is a visual metaphor, taken from the world of things located in space. It requires us to imagine the upper surface of our being versus the depth that lies under it. In contrast, "voices" is an auditory metaphor that requires us to imagine meanings as object-less voices coming from elsewhere.

To combine these two metaphors, we may say that our inner depth is the "place" within us where we can "hear" the voices of reality. In this sense, contemplating from our inner depth is approximately the same as listening to the voices of reality.

7a. Realness within
(Reflection on Pillar 7: Transformation)

When we contemplate, we often experience a heightened sense of realness, and this is an indication that our mental states have been transformed. In everyday life, we sense material objects as real when, for example, we can touch them and they offer resistance to our touch. If my hand goes effortlessly through what seems like a wall, then it is an illusion, not a real wall. This kind of material realness is external in two senses: First, we encounter the object outside ourselves, or more precisely outside our sense-organs – outside our eyes for instance. Second, we perceive only the external surface of the object. We can never experience a wall or a tree from its inwardness (if "inwardness of a wall" means anything at all).

But the realness we sometimes experience in contemplation is internal. We experience it within us, often flooding us with its intense presence. A material object can never enter me and fill my inner depth in the same way. Its realness will always remain the external realness of an object of perception.

Inner realness is the realness we seek in Deep Philosophy. This inwardness is impossible to capture in ordinary words, which are designed for public, external objects. We therefore use a metaphor – "a wave in the ocean." Like a wave that senses the movements of the ocean within itself, we sense the meanings we contemplate as rising within our inner depth, and thus as real in a special way.

7b. Between the wave and the ocean
(Reflection on Pillar 7: Transformation)

We use the metaphor of "a wave in the ocean" to refer to the contemplator's transformed sense of realness, but also to the transformed relationship between the contemplator (the wave) and the reality which he is contemplating (the ocean). This transformed relationship has several characteristics.

First, just as a wave is not separate from the movements of the ocean's water, in an analogous way I am not separate from the reality I sense. Reality's fundamental meanings (the ocean's movements, so to speak) appear within me, and I don't need to observe them from a distance. We may say that one important characteristic of being a wave in the ocean is that I find reality within me.

A second characteristic is that it is a relationship of participation. As a contemplator, I participate in the reality which I am contemplating because I am part of it, and my movements mingle with its movements. This is different from the thinking-about relationship, where I and the object of my thought are separate and independent of each other.

A third characteristic is that being a wave in the ocean is an epistemic relation, in other words, a relationship of knowing or understanding. But as opposed to the ordinary form of knowing by representation (having in mind a representation of), this is *knowing by embodying*: I understand certain fundamental meanings because they are embodied within me. Just as a wave discovers within itself, so to speak, the movements of the ocean – its tide, underwater currents, eddies – in an analogous way I discover the meanings (or voices) of reality within me, even though I do not think-about them.

A fourth characteristic is that as a wave, I relate to the ocean through a different aspect of my being. Since the ocean's movements (or meanings) do not come to me through the channel of thinking-about, they appear in those dimensions of my being which lie outside my normal thinking psychological structures, and which we call inner depth. That is why in contemplation, when we listen inwardly to our inner depth, we feel as if our understanding floods our entire being.

In sum, through contemplation I come to relate to human reality in a fundamentally different way. I am no longer just a psychological thing in a world of things, but am transformed for the duration of the session into a wave in the ocean.

Again, this transformation is always partial. Just as you do not completely lose yourself in the novel you are reading – in the back of your mind you know that you are sitting in your armchair with a book in your hand, likewise in philosophical contemplation we typically maintain the awareness of ourselves as separate individuals sitting in a room and performing contemplation exercises. We are transformed in some aspect of our being, and yet we remain the same in another; which is probably as much as a human being can hope for.

7c. Transformation beyond the session
(Reflection on Pillar 7: Transformation)

Philosophical contemplation can transform us while we are contemplating, but this may not be entirely satisfying. We also wish to transform ourselves beyond the session. We want to remain connected to our inner depth.

Our normal life is governed by psychological mechanisms of thought, emotion and behavior, which follow typical psychological patterns like an automatic pilot. As a result, our mental life is superficial and fragmented, while the deeper dimension of our being is largely dormant, inactive, and consequently undeveloped. Therefore, our ability to connect to what is real in us is limited.

The need to transform our inner life and transcend our superficial existence was recognized by many philosophers throughout history. Those thinkers, whom we call "transformational philosophers," include Plato, the Stoics, Spinoza, Rousseau, Nietzsche, Emerson, and many others. Although they used diverse concepts and theories, they all agreed that we are normally imprisoned in narrow and rigid psychological structures, and consequently live on the surface of life. With the help of philosophizing, however, we can take a step out of this prison, whether a small or a large step, briefly or for a longer period of time, and live a fuller life.

Especially relevant to us are those philosophers who understood inner transformation in terms of connecting to a special inner source of inspiration or wisdom – "the guiding principle" of Marcus Aurelius, "the higher self" of Novalis, "the natural self" of Rousseau, "the Over-Soul" of Emerson, and so on. For them, inner transformation meant learning to be attentive to this inner source, to awaken it and cultivate it. Despite terminological and theoretical differences among those thinkers, they all held that we can somehow learn to live "from" that inner source.

Like those philosophers, in Deep Philosophy we want to cultivate our inner depth beyond the session, in our everyday life. To do so, we work to awaken our inner depth by encouraging it to "speak" within us and express itself. As our inner depth becomes more active, we can return to it more easily and fully during the day.

One could call this "self-transformation," but this expression might be misleading. If "self-transformation" means completely changing yourself, if it means acquiring a new personality or liberating yourself from all psychological mechanisms, overcoming all emotional and behavioral patterns and becoming a totally new person, then this is an unrealistic dream. The eucalyptus will always remain a eucalyptus – it will never become a rose. The vast majority of people are destined to continue experiencing the brute power of their psychological mechanisms for the rest of their lives. Some psychological changes are certainly possible, whether through psychotherapy, or self-reflection, or maturation throughout the years, but as valuable as these changes may be, they are local and limited, and do not amount to a complete change of personality, or liberation from all psychological mechanisms.

In fact, many of our psychological structures play an important role in our lives. You cannot function without the structures that control hunger and thirst, without the linguistic structures that compose and decipher sentences, the thinking structures that plan and analyze, the emotional structures that regulate your feelings, or the structures governing social awareness and interaction.

Indeed, even after many sessions of philosophical contemplation, many of our old patterns and tendencies will remain the same, but with one important difference: Now they will not be our sole source of thoughts, feelings and behavior. An additional dimension of our being will now be more awakened. This additional dimension is what we call our inner depth.

Thus, cultivating our inner depth does not mean annihilating our psychology and replacing our personality. It means, rather, that in addition to our ordinary psychological apparatus, we now have a deeper source of life. And for certain periods of time, this deeper source may influence or even guide our various psychological forces and mechanisms.

As our inner depth awakens and grows, our psychological patterns will no longer be independent blind forces. Instead, they will become integrated and consolidated around a new inner center which will guide and direct them, for longer or shorter periods of time. My awakened inner depth will not replace who I am, but it will bring me together, center me and expand me, and at times connect me to deeper roots and greater horizons.

Part D

THE PRACTICE OF DEEP PHILOSOPHY

Philosophical contemplation requires a special state of mind, and for this reason it cannot be practiced in the casual setting of an ordinary conversation. Special methods are needed to push aside our automatic thinking patterns and open an inner space of deep listening. Special procedures are also needed to create the flow and rhythm that help create a contemplative atmosphere in the group.

Beginners often note that in contemplative sessions they are required to speak in ways that do not feel "natural." This is very true. Certainly, if you are asked to repeat the same sentence several times again and again, or read a text very slowly word by word, or limit what you say to a condensed poetic sentence, then this is very different from ordinary discourse. Contemplation requires precisely "unnatural" ways: a highly organized interaction, a flowing rhythm of activity, a mind that is focused and attentive, and careful deliberate speaking.

Chapter 10

THE GENERAL SETTING

The structure of a session

We practice Deep Philosophy primarily in groups, although many of us practice individually too. A group typically consists of about 5-12 participants, and it meets once a week for three or more sessions of about 90 minutes. Sessions are led by a facilitator who is an experienced practitioner. Although the activities in a session depend on the facilitator's personal style, they tend to have a similar basic structure and to use techniques from a common repertoire.

The effectiveness of a contemplation session depends, among other things, on the participants' state of mind and sense of togetherness. In order to maintain these, the session's focused structure is crucial. A steady, quiet, flowing activity fosters the contemplative atmosphere, while any interruption in the flow – unclear instructions, confusion about whose turn it is to speak, an abrupt change – might pull the participants out of their contemplative state of mind. The contemplative state of mind is precious but fragile. Structure, therefore, is essential.

A session typically begins with a short and focused introduction by the facilitator, who briefly explains the selected philosophical text. Depending on the text and on personal style, the introduction may be as short as a couple of sentences, or – if the text is difficult – as long as 10 minutes or even more, in which the central ideas are explained.

The session ends with a short conclusion – usually a few minutes of looking back at the session and sharing insights and experiences.

The middle of the session consists of text-contemplation. It takes up most of the meeting, and is carefully constructed by the facilitator. It consists of a sequence of exercises, designed to direct the participants to think and communicate from their inner depth. These exercises can be generally divided into three kinds: exercises for a first encounter with the text, for contemplating on the text, and for giving voice to one's personal insights.

In the first kind of exercises participants encounter the text for the first time. Here the emphasis is on understanding the text, including understanding difficult words and sentences and identifying central ideas. This is usually done through the semi-contemplative procedure of "interpretive reading" in which participants read passages from the text several times again and again, while adding their own brief interpretations, yet in a flowing way that promotes the contemplative spirit. Here is the opportunity for the facilitator to make important interpretive comments to help elucidate the text.

The second kind of exercises is used in the middle part of the session, where the focus shifts from trying to understand the text to contemplating on it from one's inner depth. Here participants resonate deeply with the ideas they have encountered. Through various exercises they create a polyphony of ideas while listening inwardly "through" the words to deeper meanings.

At this point, when participants are deep in the text and in the contemplative spirit, they are ready for the third kind of exercises in which they express their own personal voice. This is the stage of creativity, of giving voice to insights that emerge from one's inner depth. This can be done effectively only after one has delved into one's inner depth, and even then it does not always happen. Deep insights are a gift from the depth, so to speak, and they may or may not come.

Giving voice can be done verbally or in silent writing. When it ends, participants may read to each other what they have written, or share glimpses of their insights in some other way. The climax of contemplation has passed now, and the group is ready for the conclusion of the session in the form of the usual round of answers to the question: "What are you taking with you from the session?"

Regardless of the specific exercises used throughout the session, the overall contemplative activity flows naturally from beginning to end like in a musical performance.

The philosophical text

At the center of every philosophical contemplation session there is a short philosophical text, selected by the facilitator from the history of philosophy. It is usually about two pages long (about 400-600 words) containing a unified philosophical idea formulated concisely and clearly. During the session participants reflect together on the text and resonate with it, and this helps to bring the group together around a common center.

The texts we use for philosophical contemplation typically express basic human situations as seen from the inside: encountering another person (in philosophy of love for example), creating or enjoying a work of art (in philosophy of aesthetics), the sense of oneself, being in nature, etc. Our texts are, in other words, about reality as encountered by us.

This choice of texts is not a coincidence. A text that expresses a human encounter allows me, as a contemplator, to place myself inside the world of the text. I can "step into" its landscape and witness it from the inside. In contrast, a text that is completely objective, that describes only an object while ignoring my encounter with it, leaves me an external observer.

It is also not a coincidence that for contemplation we use only texts that are philosophical. We do not use poetry or history books, for example, because such texts focus on particular people, particular objects, particular events, as opposed to focusing on general fundamental meanings, which are the subject matter of philosophy. When I contemplate on an appropriate philosophical text, I can step into the realm of fundamental meanings and explore it from the inside.

The facilitator

The facilitator is a participant who leads the contemplation session of Deep Philosophy. He or she prepares the text for contemplation, opens the session by explaining to the group whatever needs to be explained, and leads the participants through a sequence of exercises. Facilitators are typically more experienced than other participants, and have been trained in the facilitation program of the Deep Philosophy Group.

Facilitators navigate the session like the captain of a ship. By giving succinct instructions and a personal example, they set the pace and the rhythm of the contemplative activity so that it flows smoothly and consistently, something that is crucial for the contemplative atmosphere, and hence for the success of the contemplation. Also, having prepared the text in advance, they can make occasional comments to help the participants understand difficult passages and note central concepts that are worth emphasizing. Therefore, in each exercise the facilitator is usually the first to speak. Often a brief comment (if the exercise allows it) can help orient the group in a fruitful direction.

In many respects, facilitation requires the art of balancing between extremes. For example, facilitators should keep their occasional comments short enough so as not to interrupt the flow, but detailed enough so as to prevent misunderstandings. They should also make their exercises open and flexible enough to allow participants to express themselves creatively, but not too open so as to lose boundaries and focus. Similarly, they should know when to end an exercise – not before participants have delved deeply into the task, but not too late so as to cause repetitiveness and boredom. These and similar tasks add up to good facilitation.

The three roles of the facilitator

Broadly speaking, the facilitator of a contemplative session has three main roles, which can be described metaphorically as: The facilitator as a tour guide, the facilitator as a music conductor, and the facilitator as a shaman.

As a tour guide, the facilitator leads the participants through the world of the text, especially in their first encounter with the text at the beginning of the session, very much as a tour guide leads tourists through the streets of a city. This includes several tasks. First, facilitators have to make sure that the participants understand difficult words in the text or ones that have a special philosophical meaning. Second, they have to point out the main "landmarks" in the "landscape of ideas" of the text. This is because participants who encounter a text for the first time, especially those with little philosophical background, often have a hard time distinguishing between central points and peripheral ideas. They may understand each sentence by itself, but fail to see how the sentences connect together into an overall landscape.

Therefore, the facilitator must make sure that the text is clear to everybody, both on the linguistic and conceptual level. Part of this clarification can be done in a short presentation of 5-10 minutes before the beginning of the contemplation, but it can also be incorporated into the contemplative exercises themselves. For example, while reading the text in the procedure of "interpretive reading," the facilitator can add brief clarifications without interrupting the flow. This can be done by offering a synonym to a difficult word, using intonation to emphasize a key phrase, reformulating and simplifying a sentence, etc.

The second role of the facilitator is, metaphorically speaking, that of a music conductor. Like a conductor who directs the musicians to create a coherent flowing music, the facilitator is responsible for the "music of ideas" produced in the group, including its rhythm, pace, and flow. These qualities are crucial for a contemplative state of mind. It is not by coincidence that music and recitation are so central in virtually all spiritual traditions, partly because they magnify the power of the words and give them a sense of special significance.

These musical effects are important in text contemplation too, because they help empower the philosophical words to resonate in one's inner depth. Differently said, they help to change the contemplator's state of mind from discursive thinking to inner listening and mental attunement to the deep meanings of the text. A good facilitator knows how to give the philosophical communication in the group those musical qualities that activate the participants' inner attention, by using an appropriate tone of voice, a slow pace, smooth transitions, as well as contemplative exercises that emphasize poetic speech or repetitive recitation of the text.

The third role of the facilitator is that of a shaman. Just as the traditional shaman mediates between the mundane human world and the world of hidden powers, likewise the facilitator mediates between the participants' mundane awareness and the deep meanings in their inner depth. Unlike a shaman, however, the facilitator does not receive special visions and powers for himself only, but rather helps participants attain them by themselves.

A good shaman-facilitator creates a sense of solemnness and wonder in the participants' minds; you cannot receive deep meanings with a casual, cynical, or light-hearted attitude, just as, by analogy, you cannot truly participate in a spiritual ritual with a playful or dismissive attitude. Using intonation and words, the facilitator inspires them to marvel at selected ideas in the text, at their depth, richness, and surprising implications. This inspires them to go beyond mere intellectual curiosity, towards an attitude of wonder in the face of the greater horizons of reality – as if they were entering a temple or a sacred space.

To create a sense of sacred space, the facilitator may briefly point out to the participants the element in the text that is remarkable, surprising, wondrous – in short, what we sometimes call the text's "fire" or "wow!" But often it is enough to emphasize an intriguing expression in the text and ask the participants to recite it or savor it in their minds, until its surface understanding opens up to deeper meanings.

Chapter 11

METHODS

Philosophical contemplation is a structured activity, designed to take us beyond normal thinking to our inner depth. Like many other kinds of focused practices – yoga, meditation, playing music, and martial arts – it requires adherence to special guidelines and methods.

A. *Exercises for the beginning of a session*

At the beginning of a session of text-contemplation, the group faces two main tasks: to start entering a contemplative state of mind, and to understand the philosophical text. The following exercises are commonly used for these purposes.

1. Centering exercise

A contemplation session typically starts with a centering exercise. This is a brief meditative technique in which the participants close their eyes and attend inwardly according to the facilitator's instructions.

The centering exercise has two main functions. First, it serves to mark the transition from the day's normal activity to the realm of contemplation. Second, and more practically, it is intended to silence the mind and prepare it for contemplation. This is because when participants sit down to start contemplating, their minds are still animated by the daily commotion, and a few minutes of winding down are required.

Centering exercises, by definition, do not deal with philosophical texts or ideas (or else they would be considered contemplative exercises). Since they are preparatory exercises, they are usually short, often lasting three to five minutes.

A variety of centering exercises are used in Deep Philosophy sessions. In some versions, participants are instructed to recall their busy activities before the session, and then gently let go of them and become present and focused.

In other kinds of centering exercises, participants use their body as a focus of attention. They may concentrate on their breath, or they may focus their attention on their head and then slowly descend along their body until they reach their feet, or they may focus on the breathing motions in their body, gently shifting their attention downwards from the nose to the mouth, throat, chest, abdomen, and so on.

In a third kind of centering exercise, participants follow the facilitator's instructions to shape their inner attitudes through a sequence of images. For example: Let go of your thoughts, open the walls that surround you, rest in the arms of the world, etc.

2. Interpretive Reading

After the centering exercise, when the mind is quiet and focused, it is time to turn to the philosophical text. Since the text is unfamiliar to most participants, it is necessary to first read it and understand it, yet without losing the contemplative spirit. The most common exercise used for this purpose is "interpretive reading," in which participants study together a new philosophical text in a semi-contemplative way.

The basic idea in interpretive reading is that each paragraph is read out loud several times (usually three or four times) by one participant after another. For the sake of uninterrupted rhythm, the order of the reading is predetermined, according to alphabetical order (in online meetings) or sitting position (in face-to-face meetings). Readers are encouraged to occasionally add their own interpretations to the text as they read it, provided they are brief and blend into the reading. They may include, for example, a synonym of a difficult word or a reformulation of a complex phrase, and their role is to clarify what the text says, without expressing personal opinions.

The facilitator is usually the first reader of each paragraph. After the facilitator finishes reading (with light interpretations) the first paragraph, another participant reads the same paragraph again, then the next participant (and then, if needed, a fourth or even fifth reader). After finishing with the first paragraph, the facilitator moves on to the second paragraph, reads it with light interpretations, and is followed by two or more readers who read the same paragraph. The next paragraph is read in a similar way, and so on until the end of the text.

As the text is being read, the participants are instructed to attend carefully to each word, to its sound and intonation, imagery and meaning. This careful listening, together with the repetitive reading of the same paragraph again and again, produce the beginning of a contemplative atmosphere. It is not yet fully contemplative, since some degree of analyzing the text is still required, but neither is it fully intellectual. It can be seen as a middle ground between discursive and contemplative thinking.

In order to deepen the contemplative atmosphere, as well as the sense of togetherness, the facilitator may introduce a brief contemplative exercise after some paragraphs: A mantra-like repetition of a selected sentence (so-called "Ruminatio"), or resonating with the text in so-called "precious speaking" (brief, poetic statements spoken in a focused way), etc.

3. Drawing a map of ideas

A more sophisticated exercise for studying a philosophical text is drawing a map of ideas. The map is intended to represent the conceptual structure of the text, or what we call its "landscape of ideas." We call it "landscape" because it is analogous to the way landmarks are organized on a geographic terrain. Just as a geographic landscape is made of hills, lakes, rivers, etc., a theory is made of several concepts that occupy specific locations in a conceptual terrain and stand in certain relations to each other.

When we draw the conceptual landscape of a theory, the result is a "map of Ideas," and the two should not be confused: A landscape of ideas is an abstract conceptual structure, while a map of ideas is a drawing on a sheet of paper (or computer screen) which represents that landscape.

Understanding the text's precise landscape of ideas is not always important in a Deep Philosophy session. But if the facilitator wishes to use this exercise in order to visualize more clearly the logical structure of the text, the text's map of ideas is usually drawn by the entire group together.

The exercise begins after the group has already read the text at least once, either in interpretive reading or in a simple quick reading. The facilitator then asks the participants to say out loud, in free order, the concepts that seem to them important in the text. To maintain the contemplative atmosphere, no explanation is allowed – a participant simply announces the concept. (Notice that a *concept* is expressed not in a full sentence, but in a word or phrase – for example, "Love," "The power of ideas," "The self," etc.).

After a few minutes, the facilitator stops and summarizes all the concepts that have been mentioned so far, usually between five and ten. This can be done by writing the concepts on a blackboard or on pieces of paper spread on the floor. In online sessions, the concepts can be written on a synchronized space such as Google Doc.

Now is the time to organize the list of concepts into a map. First, words that are similar to each other are unified. (For example, "Love" and "Loving" may both be written as "Love.") Then, the facilitator asks which of the concepts deserves to be at the center of the map, which concepts are second in importance and should be placed around the center, and how they should be related to each other. Lines can be drawn to indicate such relations. Following the participants' brief suggestions, the concepts are moved around until a satisfying map of ideas is achieved.

Clearly, this exercise cannot be fully contemplative. It requires a considerable degree of analytic thinking, as well as question-answer communication. For this reason it is best to conduct it at the beginning of the session, before delving fully into contemplation.

B. *Contemplative exercises*

After participants have understood the text and have entered a contemplative state of mind, it is time to delve into contemplation more fully. The following exercises are the main ones we use.

4. Precious speaking

Precious speaking is an important procedure in which participants give voice to their insights in a contemplative way. In order to nurture the contemplative spirit, they must listen inwardly as they articulate their insights briefly, concisely and carefully. They must also attempt to speak from their inner depth as much as they can, expressing insights that are alive in them, and pushing aside their opinions. This focused, spontaneous yet attentive way of speaking changes one's state of mind, making it more deeply contemplative.

The procedure is based on several rules of speaking and rules of listening. The standard rules of speaking are: First, whenever you speak, speak concisely and without repetition or redundancy, limiting yourself to one sentence. Second, treat each one of your words as if it is a precious gem, like a valuable gift to the group. Third, always give voice to what is alive in you at the moment, and not to already-familiar opinions. Fourth, when you react to the ideas of companions or of the text, always resonate *with* them instead of speaking *about* them. In particular, do not judge them, evaluate them, agree or disagree, but rather let your words echo with the words of the others as if you were a singer singing in a choir together with your fellow singers.

The standard rules of listening are: First, listen carefully when others speak, and remember that listening is no less important than speaking. Second, when others speak, avoid reacting in your mind by agreeing or disagreeing. Simply open an inner space of listening, and let the words enter it.

There are different versions of precious speaking, depending on the goal. In an open version, the facilitator asks the participants to freely resonate with any sentence or idea from the paragraph that has touched them. In a more focused version, the facilitator formulates a question to which the participants respond concisely. In a more personal version, the facilitator asks the participants to recall a recent experience of some specified type, and then speak "from" it in precious speaking. In a stricter version, participants are asked to complete a sentence which the facilitator starts. Sometimes they are asked to respond immediately without time to think, so their response would bypass the level of conscious thinking and express pre-formulated ideas.

The order of speaking in these exercises may vary too. According to one version, participants speak only in their turn (according to sitting position, or in alphabetic order). According to the no-order version, participants may speak whenever they feel that an idea "wants" to speak within them. When sitting in a circle, the participants can use a talking object (a smooth stone, for example), so that one may speak only when holding it.

5. Ruminatio (Recitation)

Ruminatio is another important contemplative group procedure. The facilitator selects one sentence from the philosophical text, preferably one that is pregnant with meaning, and the participants recite it over and over again, one participant after another, according to a pre-determined order. The recitation continues for several rounds, sometimes for five or even more minutes. While waiting for their turn to speak, participants listen carefully to the other participants' recitation, savoring the words and avoiding distractions.

When we recite a sentence over and over again, after a while the words start losing their ordinary meaning. We no longer hear just the idea conveyed, as we do in ordinary conversations, but also the words themselves – their sounds, their rhythm, their intonation. Also, our thinking is no longer discursive and logical, and we become attentive to all kinds of associations and hidden meanings. Often, specific phrases attract our attention, and they raise images and insights in our minds.

The exercise should be practiced after the group has studied and understood a portion of the text, and now wishes to delve into it more deeply. This ensures that the selected sentence is not misunderstood, because the participants have already understood the text in which it is embedded.

6. Gentle reading

Gentle reading is an exercise of reading a philosophical text very slowly, receptively, and with a special attention to each word, so as to break the mind's ordinary reading pattern. It can be practiced either individually or in a group.

In the individual version, you sit quietly and read the text much more slowly than usual, savoring the words and the ideas as they float through your mind, careful not to impose on them any interpretation. All thoughts, eye movements and bodily movements are gentle and flowing, without effort or abruptness, whether you turn a page, open a dictionary, or improve your seating position.

While reading gently in this way, you also listen carefully to ideas and images that may surface in your mind in response to the text. It is as if the text wants to speak in your mind, and you therefore vacate for it the inner space it needs. Occasionally a word or a phrase in the text will attract your attention, and then you may gently read it several times and listen to it speak in you.

In the group version, too, each participant reads silently, as in the individual version, but the pace is determined by the facilitator, who indicates the beginning of each sentence by reading out loud its first words. For example, the facilitator may read out loud the first word of the first sentence, then wait silently for a few seconds while the participants read gently the rest of the sentence, then read out loud the beginning of the second sentence, wait a few seconds, and so on until the end of the paragraph. Alternatively, the facilitator may simply instruct the participants to take a few minutes to read silently and gently a selected paragraph.

After the gentle reading, the participants may share, in precious speaking or in some writing exercise, the phrases in the text that touched them, as well as the insights which appeared in their minds.

7. Gentle writing

In gentle writing we contemplate on a short philosophical text while copying it onto a page precisely and carefully, making the hand's writing movements present to the mind. The movements of the fingers and of the pen become intensely present, and one often experiences them with fascination as if they are moving by themselves. The mind, focused on the shaping of each letter, transcends its automatic thinking mode and listens to the words of the text "speaking" and eliciting ideas or images.

Gentle writing can be especially effective when writing in calligraphy. There is no need to be a professional calligrapher to do so. What matters is not the professional result but the process of careful writing.

8. Free-floating reading

This procedure, too, is designed to break our automatic thinking patterns. Here we read a philosophical text, or listen to it being read, with a relaxed mind and without trying to capture its ideas in our understanding. Effortlessly we let the words and ideas float through our mind.

In the individual version, we relax our mind and read the text slowly and gently, letting the words flow without any mental effort to understand them.

In the group version, the text is read out loud by the facilitator (or by another participant who is a good reader), while the other participants listen effortlessly with their eyes closed. Listening with your eyes closed may make it difficult to follow the text, but the listeners do not struggle to understand it – they simply let the words flow through their mind. They will likely miss some of the ideas, but they will notice glimpses of thoughts, images, and insights. The result will be a different kind of understanding – fragmentary, vague, beyond logical structure, modest and yet deep.

After the exercise, the participants may share in precious speaking their personal insights from the text.

9. Guided philosophical imagery

In the procedure of guided philosophical imagery we explore a short philosophical text through visual imagery. The participants imagine themselves entering the world described by the text and exploring various regions or aspects of it. This allows them to give voice to the non-verbal aspects of the insights received from the text.

The philosophical text in this exercise must be appropriate for visualization. Examples are Plato's Allegory of the Cave (sitting in a cave, then standing up and walking towards the exit), Nietzsche's three metamorphosis (the camel, lion and child), or Bergson's metaphor of our inner life as a lake covered by dead leaves.

Before starting, the participants read the text to understand its basic ideas, using a text-learning procedure such as interpretive reading. Then the facilitator instructs them to close their eyes and imagine themselves in a certain place in the world described by the text (for example, sitting in Plato's cave, or standing by Bergson's lake). Next, they are asked to start moving in a certain direction, or towards some destination (walk out of Plato's cave, for example, or dive into Bergson's lake, etc.). Silently they imagine themselves on that journey, noticing the changing landscape and encountering various objects, whatever their imagination produces. After five minutes or more, the facilitator instructs them to stop, turn around and begin going back to the starting point. Once they are back, they gently leave the imagined world and return the room.

It is now time to put in words some of the experiences they had encountered and share them with the group. This can be done in various procedures such as precious speaking, writing a philosophical group-poem, or drawing.

10. Opening a door to the Depth

By "Door to the Depth" we mean a fragment of a philosophical text – usually a sentence or phrase – which is pregnant with meanings and points us beyond the surface to a deeper understanding. The fragment acts like a traffic sign that tells the reader not to stop at the surface understanding of the words, but to look further "through" it to the depth that hides beyond it.

Typically a door to the depth includes an idea that we cannot fully encompass in our mind, thus inviting us to search more deeply. It strikes us as making sense, yet we find ourselves unable to translate it fully into a definite thought. Like a three-dimensional object that cannot be flattened onto a two-dimensional shadow, it refuses to be exhausted by any linguistic summary. Nevertheless it somehow touches us as meaningful, and thus calls us to understand it in some other way, in our inner depth.

The exercise of door to the depth can be used in contemplative sessions to direct participants to attend inwardly. The facilitator instructs the participants to read the text silently, slowly and gently, and try to identify a phrase or sentence that acts for them as a door to the depth, in other words that "invites" them to delve deeper and attend to hidden meanings.

Once a participant identifies a door, he or she shares it with the group by reading it out loud. Other participants may then resonate with that door by repeating it, or by adding to it a brief interpretation or elaboration. In this way they delve together into its meaning and enrich it. After a few moments of resonating, the participants may continue reading the text and sharing additional doors.

11. Speaking out of an experience

Several exercises enable participants to resonate with philosophical ideas in a personal way, by connecting these ideas to a recent personal experience. This can help make the text more concrete and personally significant.

One such exercise is "speaking out of an experience." The facilitator asks the participants to close their eyes, reflect, and select a recent experience that is connected with a given idea in the text. For example, if the text is about togetherness, the facilitator may ask the participants to select a recent situation in which they experienced a sense of togetherness with somebody. Or, if the text is about the meaning of silence, to select a moment in which they felt deep inner silence; and so on.

Next, each participant gives a short title to their selected experience (a phrase or a word), and writes it down. If a common writing space is available (like Google Doc in online sessions), participants can also add a brief poetic sentence related to the experience. No objective information about the experience should be given to others.

After this preliminary stage, the heart of the exercise begins. As in precious speaking, the facilitator asks a question related to the topic (for example: "What happens to me when I am in togetherness?"), or starts a sentence for participants to complete (for example: "In a moment of silence in nature, I realize that..."). Participants respond out loud, freely and without order, whenever a meaningful response appears in their mind. Importantly, however, they are instructed to speak *from* their selected experience, not *about* it. To do so, they immerse themselves each in his or her personal experience and express themselves as if they are experiencing it right now. An example might be: "When I look at your face, I feel that no distance separates us from each other."

The participants keep speaking *from* their respective experiences for a few minutes. The facilitator can then present another question that highlights a different perspective on the same topic, and then a third question. Although the participants know very little about each other's experiences, the result is a rich group-polyphony on a common theme.

12. Enrichment (Enriching a personal experience)

This exercise, too, is designed to connect ideas from the philosophical text to personal experiences. Unlike the previous exercise, however, here the entire group focuses on the experience of one person, and enriches it by resonating with it.

The facilitator first asks everybody to select a recent experience related to the text (for example, a moment of being struck by a sense of the sublime, if the text is about the sublime). One volunteer then says a couple of sentences *from* that experience (as opposed to describing it from the outside), for example: "Looking at the endless forests around me, I sense that I am a particle in the infinite space." The others then resonate with this experience by speaking *from* it, as if they themselves are experiencing it now, adding to it additional facets and thus enriching it. Importantly, they do not try to guess what the volunteer in fact experienced, because that is no longer relevant. They are now constructing together a new imaginary experience, which, though rooted in the volunteer's personal experience, does not have to be faithful to it. The result is a rich network of ideas and meanings surrounding the selected experience.

If time allows, the group may then move to the experience of a second volunteer and enrich it too.

C. *Integrating and concluding the session*

After about an hour of text-contemplation, using some of the above exercises, it is time to start concluding the session. Here we want participants to look back at the session as a whole, voice their personal responses, and share with others what they have experienced.

13. Voicing

Voicing is a contemplative procedure which allows participants to give voice to their own philosophical vision, in the form of a personal response to the text as a whole. It therefore requires more creative thinking and self-expression than the exercises described above. It is usually practiced in writing, in order to allow a fuller development of one's personal voice. The exercise is typically practiced towards the end of the session, after the group has already immersed itself into the text and has a deeper understanding of what it says.

Most of the exercise is practiced individually, but in the presence of the group. All sit silently together and reflect inwardly on the text which by now they know well, either with their eyes closed or gently hovering over the text. The facilitator may ask a guiding question to focus their reflection.

In their free time, participants notice insights that surface spontaneously in their awareness, and then write them down in several lines of concise and poetic words. In face-to-face sessions they may each write on a separate sheet of paper, while in online sessions they may write on the group's shared document (such as Google Doc). Even in online sessions, however, it is sometimes helpful to first write on a personal sheet of paper and only then copy the words to the shared document on the computer screen. This is because the physical writing process itself has a contemplative power, since the careful drawing of letters on paper helps keep the mind focused and quiet, and to release further insights.

Unlike ordinary writing, voicing is done while participants are still in the contemplative state of mind achieved earlier in the session. To maintain this contemplative state, the writing is done in a precise and poetic style. As a result, the writing expresses a deeper voice within the writer, beyond normal discursive thinking patterns. In this respect, voicing is similar to the procedure of precious speaking, but the two are also different in important respects: In the procedure of precious speaking you react to an idea that is provided to you by the text, while in voicing you are the source of the ideas and are free to give shape to your own philosophical insights. And since in voicing you can write several sentences – as opposed to one single sentence in precious speaking, you can develop your insights more fully and creatively.

Thus, voicing can be seen as the highest stage of a contemplative activity: After studying a text and delving into its network of ideas, and after contemplating on it by resonating with it and with your companions, you are now a deep philosopher yourself, creatively giving voice to your own vision.

14. Group poem

This exercise, too, is practiced towards the end of the session, after the group has studied the entire text and contemplated on it. It is similar to the exercise of voicing, with the main difference that here the participants write one common text. To do this, each participant writes two poetic lines, and everybody's lines are then joined together into one unified group poem, thus expressing the spirit of togetherness.

To start the exercise, the facilitator asks the participants either to close their eyes and recall the text as a whole, or to read the text again gently and quietly. While doing so, they are to attend inwardly to insights that might surface in their minds. After this short reflection, the facilitator requests each one to formulate his or her insight in a poetic form, in a two-line verse, as if writing part of a poem.

The participants now fall silent as they are engaged in writing for several minutes. The contemplative state of mind is enhanced by the poetic nature of the writing, because poetic thinking channels the mind to listen to the flow of the words and images.

After about five minutes, when everybody has finished writing, the participants collect their respective poetic lines and place them one under the other, thus combining them into one group poem. In an online session, this can be done on a shared document such as Google Doc. In a face-to-face meeting, the participants write on small pieces of paper which are then placed together on the floor or a table at the center of the circle.

Finally, the group poem as a whole is read out loud several times, and the participants may suggest adjustments in pronouns or tenses so as to make the text more coherent and flowing.

15. Philosophical drawing

In this exercise, too, participants resonate with the text as a whole, but by drawing on a sheet of paper instead of writing. This enables them to give voice to insights which are not easy to articulate in words.

To start the exercise, the facilitator instructs the participants to silently and gently reflect on the text as a whole, and then express their encounter with the text in a drawing. In order to avoid conceptual thinking, the drawing should be abstract, without identifiable objects (a heart, for example, or a sun), and without writing.

When the participants have finished, they place their drawings on a central table, or on chairs around the room, as if in an art exhibition. They walk freely around the room and inspect the drawings. In order to create active interaction, the facilitator places an empty sheet of paper next to each drawing, and asks the participants to write a proposed title for each picture. This is intended to serve as feedback about the meanings that might be hidden in the drawing, which even its creator may not have noticed. Afterwards they all sit down again, show each other their drawing, read out loud the proposed titles received from the group, and explain their original intention.

This exercise is designed for face-to-face groups, and is difficult to practice in an online session.

16. What am I taking with me?

Before ending the session, it is a good idea to spend the last few moments looking back at the session as a whole and sharing with others what we have received from it. This is the role of the simple procedure of "What am I taking with me?"

The facilitator formulates a summarizing question such as "What are you taking with you from the session?" and the participants respond briefly and in free order, sharing the ideas, insights and experiences that have touched them.

Chapter 12

AFTER THE SESSION

A session of philosophical contemplation lasts only about ninety minutes, more or less. What happens to us after it ends?

Recollections

During the contemplative session we experience a special sense of presence, preciousness and realness, and we hope that it would not completely disappear after the session. The experience itself will probably not continue for long, certainly not with the same intensity, but the point is not the pleasurable sensation itself. We want to preserve the awareness of the deeper dimension of our being.

That is why we practice recollections during the week. The English word "recollection" can be understood in several ways: Literally it means remembering, but the idiom "recollecting yourself" means becoming aware of yourself and of the world around you. Lastly, in a non-standard reading it can also be construed as re-collecting yourself – collecting yourself again. In this combined sense, when we recollect, we stop for a few minutes our busy activity in the world, collect our fragmented self and center it, and thus remember our inner depth.

Recollection is a short exercise – usually between five minutes and an hour – which a Deep Philosophy practitioner may practice individually several times a week. The goal of the exercise is to reconnect with our inner depth, and to remember and refresh our yearning for it and commitment to pursue it. The practice of recollection counteracts our human tendency to lose ourselves in the busy activities of the day and in the avalanche of words that constantly assails us. It counters our tendency to forget what is precious in us and to us.

The minimal form of recollecting is stopping for a few minutes our daily activity and returning to our inner silence. If this is all we do, we are still at the level of "basic recollection," because it is not yet philosophical. Doing philosophy means reflecting on fundamental ideas. For a recollection to be philosophical, it must also include a content that is philosophical, usually in the form of a brief philosophical text.

A philosophical recollection may vary in length. In a short philosophical recollection we may simply recite a selected sentence from a philosophical text that we have recently encountered and that intrigues or touches us. In a longer recollection we may practice gentle reading or writing of a paragraph or two. In an even longer recollection we may contemplate on a page or more from a philosophical text.

After the recollection, it is helpful to take a few moments to reflect on what has happened and formulate in words what you have received from the exercise – an insight, a powerful sentence, an experience, an image. It is also helpful to periodically let somebody else read your recollection report in order to provide another perspective on it. For example, you may send your weekly report to a companion who is your usual "reader," who can then react to you in writing.

Recollection 1: Gentle reading

Sitting in my office, I finish the first task of the morning, then I make an urgent phone call and jot down a memo.

Now I stop. I don't want to jump to the next task right away. I must stop and sense the silence and the depth, even if only for a few minutes. When I rush from project to project, from conversation to conversation, from one task to another – life is barely here with me, hardly real, like a fast-forwarded movie. Let me be present for a little while and sense the realness of my being, and that of the greater horizons.

I sit down on a chair by the window, a philosophical essay of Emerson in my hands: The Over-Soul. I know this text quite well, so I open it at random and select an arbitrary paragraph.

I close my eyes for a few moments, as a little ritual of entering a sacred space. For a minute or two I follow my breaths as they gradually become slower and calmer.

I now open my eyes and let them rest on the paragraph I had selected. Gently I let them glide over the lines very slowly, and I savor each word. My automatic mind does not like this slowness – it wants to run forward; it gets easily bored when it doesn't get its usual stimulations. I don't fight it, but I ignore its demands and gently keep my focus on the words and the images. I listen to the flow of ideas without imposing on them my interpretations. I am a silent witness now, a receptacle of ideas, and it is not for me to make statements. By now, my smart opinions have subsided almost completely, and I let the text speak within me as it floats through my mind.

The words keep flowing with a special precious significance. Emerson's statements are no longer mere statements but wondrous meanings from elsewhere: the Over-Soul, the universe, the hidden source.

When I finish the paragraph I go back to the beginning and read it again, and then once more.

The stillness fills me now. A big insight grows inside me, powerful yet vague, almost ineffable, and I savor it in silence for a little while until it fades away. Then I gather myself, collect my thoughts, and carefully examine my insight. I formulate a few sentences as a memory from that insight and write them down in my journal, before standing up and returning to work.

Recollection 2: Philosophical note

I know that today will be a busy day, so before going to work I devote a few minutes to reading a new page from the philosophical book on my desk: Karl Jaspers' *Way to Wisdom*. I do not have the time and peace of mind to really contemplate, but I try reading a few paragraphs as receptively as I can. I taste the words and listen to them carefully.

Then I notice the sentence: "Philosophy is the decision to awaken our original source, to find our way back to ourselves, and to help ourselves by inner action." I stop to think: What does "original source" mean? And what is the way back to myself? I do not yet fully understand the sentence, but it seems to want to tell me something. Yes, this will be my sentence for today.

I pick an index card from the pile on my desk, and I carefully copy a sentence on it. My handwriting is typically sloppy and irregular, but now I make a special effort to write as beautifully as I can.

It is late already. I quickly fold the card, place it in my shirt pocket and rush to leave the house. In the bus I disconnect my mind from the noise around me, take the card out of my pocket and slowly read the sentence several times. Once in the office, I completely forget Jaspers, and only towards noon I remember him again. At lunch break I glance at my sentence again and whisper it several times.

Again I plunge into my work, and for a long time my mind is full of urgent matters. But two hours later, as I hurry along the corridor, a few words from Jaspers surface in my mind: "Philosophy is the decision to awaken my original source." And immediately a bubble of insight follows: "My original source is the soil on which I grow."

The insight feels deep and significant, and for a few moments I reflect on it, but I do not fully understand it yet. It seems like a banality, yet it is also deeper than my mind can grasp. I write it down on a piece of paper so as not to forget. Tonight, after I get back home, I will reflect on it – perhaps even contemplate – and develop it into a little philosophical poem.

Recollection 3: Calligraphic contemplation

This afternoon I finally have some time for myself, and I decide to contemplate for a little while. I have been outside myself for three or four days, talking endlessly with co-workers, neighbors and friends. I need to be silent now – not merely to stop talking, but to submerge myself in a silent sea of inner listening. I want to regain myself and recollect.

I pick a small book which I find inspiring, a spiritual philosophical book by a favorite thinker. I sink into my armchair and start reading. Soon, however, I realize that the words do not take me to the depth. My mind is still distracted from the busy morning, and it goes through the words mechanically, without reaching the fullness of the words, the sounds of the syllables, the images, the flow of ideas. No, I need a contemplative exercise to suspend the words and give them full presence, so that I could savor them inwardly in my inner depth.

I look again at the page and select a short paragraph that impresses me as pregnant with meaning. Then I get my calligraphic pen and start copying carefully the sentences on a nice sheet of paper in calligraphic script. I am not a professional calligrapher, and my calligraphic writing is far from pretty, but when I slowly form the letters with precision, paying attention to each pen-stroke, to every line and curve, then all becomes engulfed in a deep intense silence. The movements of my fingers, the gliding motion of the pen, the lines on the paper, all are intensely present, together with the wondrous meanings that arise from the text. It is not I who is composing these meanings, but something deeper is doing it through me.

Recollection 4: Inner conversation with a text

Yesterday I received a new book by the Spanish thinker Maria Zambrano, and today I start reading it. The first few pages leave me intrigued and a little confused. The text is obscure, blurred by mists of metaphors and images. Nevertheless, several ideas strike me as potentially deep, and I want to converse about them with the writer – yes, to converse with Zambrano herself, even though she died decades ago.

A conversation with a dead thinker, as if she was alive and sitting right here with me, can be valuable. The act of conversing puts my mind in a special attitude: openness to the voice of the other. My thoughts are no longer just my own private thoughts – they transcend my separate self and move between me and the other person. Why not do the same with dead Zambrano?

I find a brief section at the beginning of the book, and I read it quietly several times, while listening internally to the ideas and images, and to my own associations and memories. And now, like in any friendly conversation, I formulate a question in my mind and silently direct it to the text, and through the text to its writer. I listen internally to the answer of Zambrano within me, and when I receive it in the form of a spontaneous bubble of thought, I reflect in silence for a while, then reply with a comment or a further question.

At first I feel a little silly speaking to a dead philosopher, but I know that at the level of inner depth, the distinctions between dead and alive and between me and another are no longer important. Deep down in the depth, there are only voices of human reality. And so I continue.

For a while, my exchange with Zambrano is somewhat forced and artificial, and it is hard to tell what is coming from my inner listening and what is coming from my mind's arbitrary inventions. But little by little the words within me gain presence and preciousness, and our communication deepens. My thoughts are now part of a larger realm of voices which give birth, every once in a while, to an insightful bubble.

Beyond recollections

After my recollection I return to the busy activity of the day, but the contemplative spirit still envelops me. Fragments of my recollections surface in my awareness every now and then, and these testify that my contemplation is not completely gone. I am in my busy self again, yet I have also received an additional dimension to my being. I am not completely the same.

But neither am I completely changed. My old psychological patterns are still active in me, but – how shall I describe it? – the world is bigger around me. I am like a traveler who has traveled to foreign lands across the seas, and is now returning to his hometown, the same person as the one who left home years ago, and yet different. My habits are the same as before, and so are my skills and my weaknesses and manner of speaking – others cannot easily detect any great difference. Yet, my world is bigger now, because I belong to greater horizons.

At times my bigger horizons are gentle like a fleeting memory, and at times they caress me with their soft presence, or inspire me with generous plenitude. Often they are so frail that their presence hardly makes any difference at all, but even then their promise remains with me and arouses deep longings. Even a mere longing makes you a different person to some extent.

I keep practicing my philosophical recollections, and once a week I participate in contemplative sessions with my companions. That is how Deep Philosophy keeps me living in a broader reality. Even when I am lost in my everyday activity, even when I get irritated or angry or tempted by silly diversions, I still have somewhere within me the knowledge that I belong to bigger dimensions. I am not just psychology, I am part of the ocean. You are not the same when you are part of something so vast.

You might call this "self-transformation," provided you remember that much of me is the same as always, and that none of the changes is final. Greater dimensions are never given to you as a final possession, only on loan. You must keep nurturing them, or else they shrivel and vanish.